A YEAR OF HOPE

A YEAR OF HOPE

LETTERS TO MY BELOVEDS

CHAPLAIN (COL) MARK NUCKOLS

Palmetto Publishing Group
Charleston, SC

A Year of Hope
Copyright © 2019 by Mark Nuckols

First Edition

Printed in the United States

Hardcover: 978-1-64111-613-8
Paperback: 978-1-64111-614-5
eBook: 978-1-64111-615-2

DEDICATION

For the precious saints who support the armed forces at home and abroad

INTRODUCTION

In July 2004, Pastor Mark Nuckols, also an Army Reserve chaplain, received a message from the US government informing him his reserve unit would soon be activated and deployed to Iraq. Only six months earlier, he had accepted a call to be shepherd of Saint Paul Lutheran Church in Austin, Texas. The thought of leaving family, friends, and his new congregation left him with great apprehension.

Just seven months after Nuckols arrived in Austin, his wife, Carla, children Mariel and Patrick, and his new flock sent him off with love and pride, albeit tears. Eager to stay connected to those he would leave behind, Pastor Nuckols began a weekly letter or epistle from the front describing his personal journey, while encouraging them to stay faithful to the Lord. These missives became a window into the realities of war, into the mission of the chaplaincy, and into the soul of a man far removed from the comforts of home and family and a loving congregation.

The letters, sent by email, were printed and distributed each Sunday to the members of Saint Paul. Through these messages of courage and faith, his readers were comforted and uplifted but also challenged to see God's work being accomplished in a distant land under difficult, sometimes harrowing, circumstances. As the days and months elapsed, the author found himself transformed as a year of dread and despair became a year of hope. Chaplain Nuckols was awarded the Bronze Star for his humanitarian work with the local villages in Iraq.

YOU'RE SENDING ME WHERE, LORD?

To my dear parish family,

By now you have heard what our good and gracious Lord is doing among us here at Saint Paul. He has allowed me to be called into active duty in the US Army and to be sent to Iraq in order to serve our soldiers as chaplain. I will be representing Saint Paul as an evangelist and missionary, and I am privileged to remain your pastor. However, since I will be unable to be present with you, Pastor Duder will be serving you until I return late in 2005. How thankful I am that you will be well cared for.

I will need your help. During this time while I'm away, continue to remain steadfast in your attendance and the study of God's Word. Invite your friends and relatives and coworkers. Let encouragement and account-ability and love reign among you that the body of Christ gathered here and around this altar may be built up in the most holy faith. Please keep in contact with my beloved Carla and with my children. They will continue to live in Kansas City until our home sells.

We know by faith in God's sure promises revealed in Word and Sacrament that He is a loving and gracious God who desires only our ben-efit. Therefore, though we do not understand what He has brought upon us, we do know by faith that He will care for us and provide all that we need to endure these events. Secondly, He would never have allowed this situation to come to pass if we were incapable of it and, ultimately, growing through it. Recall what our loving Father has proclaimed through Saint Paul; "My grace is sufficient for you. For my power is made perfect in weakness. Therefore, lift your drooping hands and strengthen your weak knees, and make straight paths for your feet, so that what is lame may not be put out of joint, but rather healed. Strive for peace with everyone, and for the holiness without which no one will see the Lord. See to it that no one fails to obtain the grace of God; that no 'root of bitterness' springs up and causes trouble, and by it many become defiled" (Heb. 12:12–15).

"Now may the God of peace who brought again from the dead our Lord Jesus, the great Shepherd of the sheep, by the blood of the eternal covenant, equip you with everything good that you may do His will, working in us that which is pleasing in His sight, through Jesus Christ, to whom be glory now and forever. Amen" (Heb. 13:20–21).

Love, Pastor Nuckols

Author's note: As I wrote those words to my flock, I realized they were meant as much for me. My heart was heavy with the burden of knowledge that I was leaving not only a new parish family but my precious wife, Carla, and children: Mariel, seventeen, full of hopes and dreams for the future as she entered her senior year of high school, and Patrick, although fifteen, still my little buddy. There were many loose ends Carla would have to handle on her own, including the selling of our home in Kansas City, seeing teenage children through another year of school, maintaining our aging vehicles, and so on. It was a time of turmoil as I faced my fears and questioned God's timing and yet also a time of sweetness as my family and I made the most of every moment together.

FIRST STOP: KUWAIT

My dear parish family,

The plane trip over to Kuwait took approximately sixteen hours, not including the almost six hours more for refueling. Our first stop was in Chicago before flying on to Keflavik, Iceland, and then to London. Finally, we landed in Kuwait City, feeling both exhausted and amped up.

Gathering our gear, we were loaded upon commercial busses and headed off to our base camp where we will await our supplies that have been transported by ship. It is our hope to be out of this camp and relocated to Iraq in about four weeks. We are becoming a very international base camp here at Camp Virginia. Soon there will be over twelve thousand soldiers occupying the smallish base. I hope we'll move on before the chaos begins!

Our installation is surrounded by a wall of dirt approximately ten feet tall, followed by a ring of barbed wire and another ten-foot wall of dirt. The land around the camp is desolate with only thorny scrub brush growing here and there. We are told to drive very aggressively but safely. Sounds like an oxymoron to me! The average citizen vehicle travels at eighty to ninety mph.

I had an opportunity to converse with various soldiers regarding our transition from home and civilian life to an unfamiliar land far from those we hold so dear. I'm thankful the Lord is opening those doors of trust. Speaking of trust, I have been comforted by the hymns from the "Trust" section of our hymnal during my daily devotions. Good stuff!

Yesterday, I broke down and purchased a collapsible chair, which will serve as my new recliner. I found a bargain, and it is much more comfortable than sitting on my cot. Sleep has been coming in spite of the time change. We have begun organized PT, and I've also been doing my own lifting in the evenings, so I'm a little sore. The mornings are mild, but by the afternoon the heat is almost unbearable. We also experienced our first sandstorm today. It lasted four hours with visibility of only several feet. The dust is very destructive to all manner of electronics. We can only use memory sticks, as floppies don't work at all and CDs must be continually cleaned.

The day we arrived, a small camel herd meandered through the camp. Due to their height and strength, we gave them a wide berth and let them move on through. I guess there are several wild herds around here, and they are often hit on the highways when drivers are distracted.

The tents we are staying in are one hundred feet by thirty-two feet. Thankfully, they are air conditioned. With generators running constantly, the spotlights aglow, and the endless moving in and out of convoys, the base takes on a carnivallike feel. We have 1.5-liter bottles of water to drink located all throughout the installation. I go through five to seven bottles a day because the heat and extremely dry conditions can cause dehydration quickly.

I am well. God has been gracious in our travels, and He continues to feed me with His Word. I will write again soon.

God's peace to you.

Love, Pastor

My dearest Carla,

Though I have been here in the "Sandbox" but briefly, my days have found a rhythm and even seem routine. For others within our unit, there are all types of missions upon which they are working, whether logistics, security, or feeding and caring for us. Even at war, it seems there are tedious days and work. I do not mean to complain, the mundane is good in a war zone, but merely describing the work patterns for now.

Sunday, I will be preaching at the general Protestant contemporary service. I chuckled to myself when I was told that they needed me to preach at this service, as you well know my convictions for our historic liturgy! The coordinator assured me that it was not necessary for me to lead it, just preach at it! I am blessed to be able to proclaim the great biblical truth of salvation by grace alone, through faith alone whenever God permits. My experiences here have not changed my theology; in fact, it has convinced me of the beauty and timelessness of our liturgy, sacraments, and hymnody. What it has done to me, however, is to soften my attitude so that I am not so exacting regarding these matters. How wonderful to hear your voice on the phone! I will try to call you at the same time more often in order to make sure I catch you all awake, coffee fueled, and ready to talk. I am so glad that it worked out that everyone was awake this morning! It was great to talk with the kids and listen to them just go on and on about whatever was on their minds! They seemed very content and enjoying school. The senior night sounded so special too. I look forward to seeing the pictures that were taken of you and Mariel when you can send them.

What great news about the Chiefs! I am so glad that you filled me in on the fine details in order for me to share with the rest of the Chiefs' fans around our tent. Go Chiefs!

A rewarding aspect of being here with so many coalition soldiers from all over the world is interacting with them in work and play. It is just like on a playground with kids of a different color or language, as it all dissolves away when you have fun together. We have been playing ping-pong with the Koreans and the Albanians, foosball with the Hungarians, cards with the Poles, and watching baseball on TV with the Japanese. That is an invaluable by-product of this mission with our allies, to build rapport and relationships with the soldiers from their nation of origin, hoping they will return home with positive experiences with their American counterparts. It is the same with the workers around here who are from Pakistan, Thailand, India, Malaysia, and other southeast Asian places too numerous and unknown to mention and, ultimately, the Kuwaitis and, of course, the Iraqis. God has His hands deep in these matters and will bring about His gloriously perfect and loving will in all things.

I, too, remarked to myself about being one with you at the table of our Lord when I received the Sacrament at service today. What a gift from God to be joined with all of you in this way. Oh, and by the way, guess which hymn we sang? We sang the hymn your mama sang to me before I deployed, "With the Lord Begin Thy Task, Jesus Will Direct It." Cool, right? We are a part of the blessed communion of saints and will NEVER be parted, one from the other. I was touched by our children's comments of wanting to receive Holy Communion at Holy Cross this Sunday as they also were thinking of me communing with them. Thank you for giving me such precious children. I am a blessed man who is continuing in his appreciation of them as well as their gifted and beautiful mother. I remember so vividly placing both Patrick and Mariel in your arms after the doctor had delivered them. Wow, what beautiful and soothing memories we have together, my dear.

Today, the scales revealed I had lost a pound! With lifting weights and replacing the fat with muscle, my overall poundage will diminish at a slower rate, so I must be patient. Lifting weights does a couple of important things for me. The physical benefit is the obvious, but it also allows me to have my mind actively engaged during the evening hours after the duty day is completed and loneliness sets in. Time is a gift, but it was meant to be used wisely and constructively by the Giver of all time. I am thankful for the upcoming busy week for our soldiers given our present "downtime" as we wait for our gear and our vehicles to arrive in country. I can tell that it is slowly taking its toll on many of them. One of the soldiers here has the Blue Collar Comedy Tour DVD on his computer, and I am laughing out loud listening to their goofy humor. It makes me think of our trip to Indiana when we listened to Patrick's CD in the Jeep as we traveled. To be with one another, to not have any other "things" pressing in upon our time, to talk together, and to laugh together, all in spite of the long distance traveled in a cramped vehicle. So fun!

Last night I was looking at the halfmoon and I said to myself, "My girl is looking at this same moon, and that means that we are not that far from one another." I was also thinking that I would like you to find a few beautiful colored leaves from some of the maples in the area and send them to me. It would give me a little bit of home and remind me of our wonderful walks and our soothing talks about any and all matters. You are my love, my best friend, and my true companion. Thank you, Carla.

I love you, Mark

My dear parish family:

Our staging camp, Camp Virginia, is growing in numbers and in nationalities each day. Our Korean allies are the predominant nationality other than US troops. It has been a blessing to get to know some of them. Most are Christians and attend the services here at camp. The great way to communicate with our coalition forces is to play with them, be it ping-pong, volleyball, soccer, or basketball. Those activities do a great service to building bridges with the rest of the world. Sort of like our playground and sports programs at Saint Paul, which mixes and integrates all our children. However, the greatest mixer of all is the common faith in our Lord Jesus Christ expressed in our ecumenical worship services. What a blessing to be able to praise God using a liturgy unto which we as Lutherans have always ascribed!

Our days here have become somewhat repetitive, or at least for me. For others within our unit, there are various missions upon which they are working. For example, some are attending a five-day class down at Camp Doha on handling the various contracts that need to be written, implemented, and paid for while we are here with the various businesses with whom we will be working in order to supply our movement units with what they need and to maintain and improve our camp at "Q-West." Even at war there are repetitive days and work!

The colonel and ten of our soldiers will be back later this week (October 28–29). It will be nice to see them again! Our facilities in Iraq will not be as rudimentary as we had expected, but we will still need to develop them further upon our arrival. Our total camp population at Q-West will be around one thousand soldiers. Here at Camp Virginia, we already have about two to three thousand soldiers. We also will enjoy a decent chow hall there at Q-West as well as an MWR tent. MWR stands for Morale, Welfare, and Recreation, with an MWR tent being like a student union on a college campus equipped with games, books, videos, and a small theater.

In order to handle our downtime, I have begun lifting weights at the makeshift gym here at Camp Virginia. Many of our soldiers have never been apart from their loved ones for more than a few days at a time, and for them, downtime can become a very lonely time. Several of them are newly married, meaning less than a year, and are now going to be apart for more than a year. Yes, pray for these soldiers, but more importantly, pray for their faith and for the faith of their spouses that they may be strengthened in order to be used by Him while they are apart from one another and when they return.

God is always beckoning us to be dependent upon Him, isn't He? Lately, during my morning and evening prayers, I have been singing hymn 409 from our blue hymnal, *Lutheran Worship*. It is called "From God Can Nothing Move Me." Especially these verses:

> *When those whom I regarded as trustworthy and sure*
> *Have long from me departed, God's grace shall still endure.*
> *He cares for all my needs, from sin and shame corrects me.*
> *From Satan's bonds protects me; not even death succeeds.*
>
> *Yet even though I suffer the world's unpleasantness,*
> *And though the days grow rougher and bring me great distress,*
> *That day of bliss divine, which knows no end or measure,*
> *And Christ, who is my pleasure, forever shall be mine*

And my Psalm of the day has been from Psalm 55, especially verses16–19 which read:

> *But I call to God,*
> *   and the Lord will save me.*
> *Evening and morning and at noon*
> *   I utter my complaint and moan,*

and He hears my voice.
He redeems my soul in safety
*   from the battle that I wage,*
*   for many are arrayed against me.*
God will give ear and humble them,
*   He who is enthroned from of old,*
because they do not change
*   and do not fear God.*

Satan is constantly seeking our demise, but since we are God's children, he is powerless to do so because of the "one little word that fells him" given to us from God's Word to speak and to cling unto. Rejoice in God's promises from of old, for they have sustained the saints who have gone before us and will sustain the saints who follow us. To God be the glory as we celebrate the one true Faith, that resides in every corner of the earth.

Love, Pastor

My dear parish family,

Services on the celebration of Reformation Day went swimmingly. Being able to sing "A Mighty Fortress" was the icing on that special day. Later that evening we had about two hundred or so gather for a camp-wide Halloween 5k fun run. Our unit alone had close to twenty-five in attendance at the start. The route inside the camp was lined with glow-in-the-dark chemical lights of red, blue, and green. When I say they lined the route, I am talking about lining both sides of the 3.1-mile road race with a chemical light every three feet! It was an unusual experience to say the least but extremely enjoyable and very pleasing to the eye. Following the run, we all partook of freshly baked pizzas and hot dogs, washing them down with ice-cold Gatorade and water. The next day, I paid for the robust exertion with which I attacked the course, but the endorphin high after the run and the comradery was well worth it!

An interesting phenomenon occurred recently. For the first time since our arrival, we had dew on the ground, on the tents, and on the vehicles. Prior to Sunday evening, there was no such occurrence around here. I am assuming that it is a part of the weather patterns here as they begin their shift into the fall and winter mode. After having such a dry climate embracing us, the feel of even the slightest of humidity is uncomfortable and not welcomed.

That humidity was all a precursor to the major storm cell that followed, blowing through the camp and radically changing our somewhat predictable lives. It all began around 10:30 p.m. Tuesday evening as a little sprinkle, which quickly turned into an all-out downpour. Our large canvas tents were not very well equipped for handling that amount of moisture; therefore, some minor dripping at the seams gave way to major leaking all around. Scurrying about, we tried to keep all of our belongings as dry as possible, but to no avail. Very strong winds were pushing the rain, and soon our tent was torn to shreds, leaving us completely exposed and equally surprised. Grabbing our essential goods, we moved to a nearby tent. Once safely sheltered, we only could watch as the remainder of our things were soaked or destroyed. By 2:30 a.m. our excitement had given way to exhaustion, and with that, we haphazardly bedded down for the night. Thanks be to God for Ziploc plastic bags and ponchos. Most of my things, especially my laptop and my guitar, were spared from the deluge.

The morning brought with it the gathering of our soaked belongings, drying them as best as possible, and moving to another set of tents while they repaired our utterly wrecked abodes. Thankfully, no one was hurt badly, although we did have one of our soldiers with a gash in his head that required two staples and another one who received a small electrical burn to his hand. And so…the rainy season has begun.

I'm writing you while I am on TOC (tactical operation center) duty from midnight until 4 a.m. following the night after the crazy storm. Our TOC is the main clearinghouse for all incoming messages and information as well as the central distribution point for all outgoing messages and information. It is manned twenty-four hours a day, and everyone serves a shift. I just happened to be "unlucky" this time and was scheduled long before the storm blew in. I have been catnapping throughout the late afternoon and into the evening in preparation for tonight's duty. Tomorrow, I will be able to catch up on my sleep since I am free for most of the day. However, we still have our nightly staff meetings. All of this is part of our new routine for the year to come.

Having received an emergency Red Cross message, we are sending one of our soldiers back to the States for a thirty-day leave in order to manage a severe family situation. We receive about two of these messages a week just for the soldiers in our unit who have situations back home needing attention. These "situations" do not always require an emergency leave to return to the States. Most of the time the soldier needs only to make several phone calls to various people and organizations in order to care for the crisis. When we are responsible for our permanent camp in northern Iraq, which will be home to around 1,500 soldiers, our TOC will be handling more than just two calls a week. Again, I am so grateful for the amazing soldiers we have serving in our armed forces in order to insure a safer America.

In my devotion this morning, I read a priceless quote by C. S. Lewis regarding feelings or sensations. His point is toward feelings that are "highs," but the quote could also be applicable for feelings that are "lows."

> All our prayers are being answered and I thank God for it. The only (possibly, not necessarily) unfavourable symptom is that you are just a trifle too excited. It is quite right that you should feel that "something terrific" has happened to you…Accept these sensations with thankfulness as birthday cards from God, but remember that they are only greetings, not the real gift. I mean that it is not the sensations that are the real thing. The real thing is the gift of the Holy Spirit, which can't usually be—perhaps not ever— experienced as a sensation or emotion. The sensations are merely the response of your nervous system. Don't depend on them. Otherwise when they go and you are once more emotionally flat (as you certainly will be quite soon), you might think that the real thing had gone, too. But it won't. It will be there when you can't feel it. It may even be operative when you can feel it least. Don't imagine it is all "going to be an exciting adventure from now on." It won't. Excitement (or one could add, sorrow or fear) or whatever sort of emotion, never lasts. This is the push to start you off on your first bicycle: you'll be left lots of dogged pedaling later on. And no need to feel depressed about it either. It will be good for your spiritual leg muscles. So, enjoy the push while it lasts, but enjoy it as a treat, not as something normal.

Here, I will add to Lewis's words: take heart during this time of separation. Enjoy the people God has placed in your lives. I am grateful for those who are serving in my absence. Know that this time apart is not normal but will pass and the ordinary will return. Until then, we all stretch our spiritual leg muscles!

We should be moving up to northern Iraq in several days. God's peace to you all, and thank you for your prayers.

Love, Your Pastor

My dear parish family,

Communications here in the Sandbox are intermittent at the present time due to the spectacular electrical storm we received last week. The harsh environment of the dust and heat also wreaks havoc on all manner of electrical equipment. There are free military phone lines available, but they are extremely limited due to the sheer number of soldiers here at Camp Virginia. The army has internet, but it is being reworked since lightning struck the transmission tower. However, with the entrepreneurial spirit of our American companies, we do have at our disposal a phone service hosted by AT&T for twenty cents a minute overseas, and in addition, there is a high-speed internet service at five dollars an hour. Yet, despite the present increase in cost, what a blessing it is to have the opportunity to hear my loved ones' voices every now and then!

At long last, our gear and vehicles, which were shipped by sea, have arrived in port and have been picked up by a forty-man detail. Having driven the vehicles to Camp Virginia, we will begin to harden them with 6 mm thick steel in order to make them more battle worthy to small arms fire and roadside IEDs (Improvised Explosive Devices). We will also be installing gun mounts in the back of several of our vehicles for our various automatic weapons systems. We will be utilizing the SAW (Squad Automatic Weapon), a 5.56 mm fully automatic machine gun; the M-60, a 7.62 mm fully automatic machine gun; and the mother of all the machine guns, the .50 caliber. In addition to these, we will also have a few 40 mm automatic grenade throwers known as the Mark 19. As you may already know, a chaplain is a noncombatant, and I carry no weapon. My chaplain assistant provides for my safety since my mission is to serve the soldiers in a religious and spiritually supportive way.

God willing, none of our soldiers will have to fire them in order to harm someone, but that is a distinct possibility given the aggressive nature of the militant insurgents. Since the insurgents cannot beat our firepower, they desire to discredit the leadership of our nation, turning this operation into another "Vietnam" so that the American people lose their desire to support the work of freedom. Be not dismayed of what you hear in most of the media, for with the help of the Iraqi people, we are accomplishing much toward freeing a nation and building the bridges of goodwill. I have seen and heard too many positive examples of our presence here to discredit that which is usually reported to you via the news networks.

Enough of my amateur analysis! Our plans as a unit to convoy up to northern Iraq will occur sometime before the end of November. In the meantime, we will be intensely focused on preparatory training for this upcoming troop movement north that will take several days.

Last Sunday I again hosted the general Protestant service. There was a unique resemblance between our small gathering and to the people of Israel. During their pilgrimage, they worshiped in a tent as they traveled from slavery in Egypt to the promised land of freedom, so we, the new Israel (the church), found ourselves worshipping in a tent as we travel from slavery in sin to the promised land of heaven. Another interesting note regarding last Sunday's service was that due to the storm last week, the electronics (PA system and hymn accompaniment) in the chapel were "fried." Therefore, we had to sing our hymns completely unaccompanied. The soldiers did a fine job of belting out the melody and sounding off louder than the hum of the two large air-conditioning units.

I've told you about my commander, who is very supportive of my work as a chaplain as well as being supportive of me as one of my "parishioners." He was just recently informed that his father had died. Thankfully, he had been able to visit with his father at length immediately prior to his departure for this mission. Because of this and other reasons, he thought it best to remain here rather than return home for the funeral. Pulling me aside, he requested that I read to him some Scripture and pray with him. So while his father's funeral was occurring in the States, we sat out here in the desert, in the dark, reading, praying, and singing. I was honored to have the privilege to bring God's Word of comfort to him. I lost my father last January, and I felt a real kinship with my commander as we worshipped and grieved together.

As you can see, you are accomplishing many things here far away from the comfort of your home by allowing me to serve our nation and our beloved church. But is God's work through you any different back home? No! God is using you in the same manner with your family, with your workplace, and with your friendships and acquaintances. He has already extended His kingdom and will continue to do the same by using such people as we. What an amazingly merciful God we call Father who would do such great things, many of which we are completely clueless about. Do not think that you have to go somewhere to do such work? No, dear friends, that is a deceptive lie by Satan and the world. God has literally brought into your backyard enough work to do to keep you busy until He calls you home. Besides, the glory of mission work can be highly overrated if we place it above the everyday interactions with those who are seeking Christ in our very midst! It is merely doing the same thing that we would do at home in a different location and without our normal support system. So keep working and remember: "...be steadfast, immovable, always abounding in the work of the Lord, knowing that in the Lord your labor is not in vain" (1 Cor. 15:58).

Love, Pastor

My dear parish family:

With the change of weather patterns comes a change in some of the wildlife around the camp here in Kuwait. I recently spied a desert fox running through our part of the camp. He was beautiful. We also have wild dogs that basically look like "junkyard mongrels," but this was a real desert animal. In addition to the fox, I have also seen some beautiful birds of prey, maybe a falcon or a small hawk flying low through the camp, probably looking for some of the fat pigeons that hang around here gobbling up tasty morsels. Songbirds are normally nonexistent; however, I did see some birds that appeared to be a desert-colored titmouse and smaller cardinal-type birds. Both had the signature tuft on the back of their heads. God's creation is amazingly diverse and well adapted to the severe environment found in this area of the world.

One of our tough young troopers, a female, has had to be sent to a hospital in Landstuhl, Germany, for an evaluation of her feet. She was heartbroken because of her great desire to stay with us as a unit. She is our shortest soldier at four feet, ten inches, but her spirit and determination are as "big as Texas." What an inspiration to the unit. We had a "God's speed" party for her before her flight to Germany on the fifteenth. She was one of my Missouri Synod Lutheran soldiers who was a regular in our services.

At our nightly command and staff meetings, my commander has asked me to give brief vignettes on the biblically historical significance of sites in and around Iraq. These talks have really opened a new door for me to share more in-depth teachings about our Lord and His great work for us. Before we left the States, I was able to put together a Power Point presentation on these matters. The colonel asked me to give the presentation to the entire group during some of our training time. Once again, to God be the glory for the opportunity He has given me to share the gospel in a very nonthreatening manner, opening the door wide for further discussions at various times and places following the presentation. God's hand is mightily at work here just as He is in your workplaces, in your home, and in your other locales of influence.

In a recent letter, I shared about a Moroccan soldier who will soon become an American citizen and how he is fluent in Arabic. Well, through some of his own research on the internet, he has come up with some great intel on the efforts of the militants. The problem with this information is that it leaves one feeling very uneasy about any convoy operations or even about being stationed here in Iraq. Pragmatically speaking, though, if this raises the awareness of the need for repetitive training for the sake of safety and success, then it could be deemed an important achievement. One of the outcomes of this presentation was the decision by some of our officers that we, as a unit, hold regular midweek prayer/devotional meetings for any and all who would like to attend as well as Sunday a.m. services specifically for our unit. As you know, the readings for this time of the church year focus on the end times. All I could think was how appropriate is our preparation for our convoy north. My, how the Holy Spirit can work upon the hearts of His people when we begin to see the frailty of our lives.

Stress can bring out the good as well as the bad in people, can't it? It has been an interesting study in human behavior to watch my fellow officers and senior NCOs handle this human emotion. Please, don't misunderstand, I have also seen the results of this feeling inside of me, and I am no different than they. Normally we do not choose to live in a stressful environment or situation, yet what does our Lord allow? At times, He places us in situations full of stress. Some of our stress has been authored by ourselves, and some has been laid upon us. But either way, God uses it to drive us to our knees in humility, seeking His strength and hope. Relationally, it can quickly strip us of our veneers of civility, and we are shown the sins of our flesh, and those of others, quite clearly. The hoped-for result is that these stressful events bring us all to repentance and reconciliation with one another so that we are enabled to handle such things cohesively rather than divisively. Slowly, these events in our lives will further shape us into a family. God willing, these soldiers, including me, will always see these events as such, for our benefit. Sounds a little like Saint Paul or the church at large, doesn't it? "May it be done unto us as You have said. We are the Lord's servants" (revised from Mary's song).

Another interesting observation of human behavior is our strong will of independence. As you know, the military is all about homogeneous apparel and consistency in all articles of clothing. Well, some of the ways in which we, as soldiers, choose to express ourselves here in theater in order to push the limits on propriety are very noteworthy. For example, for females, their hair can be any length as long as they pin it up in a bun of some sort while they are on duty. There are ten to fifteen young ladies here at this camp of about seven thousand soldiers who have decided to be totally different and buzz cut their hair off. Although there are prohibitions against females having hair that measures too long, there are none addressing the wearing of hair too short! Another example of individuality is in the wearing of our soft caps, which resemble baseball caps. Many of our young soldiers enjoy rolling them a little on top in order to make them look just a little different but still within regulations. They call it wearing the cap "Ranger style."

Within the week, I will have a permanent address for our camp in northern Iraq. I will send that information in my next email.

God's peace to you.

Love, Pastor

PART III:
CONVOY TO IRAQ

My dear parish family,

By the time you read this, my unit will be at our final destination in northern Iraq. We will be standing up a new supply hub for the entire northern sector of Iraq. From Camp Virginia, Kuwait, to our final home of Q-West, Iraq, is about six hundred miles. It will take us approximately three full days to travel that distance as a convoy of vehicles. Our second day of traveling will be spent navigating through Baghdad with its attendant difficulties. I will be the primary driver of my vehicle in our convoy of twenty-plus vehicles. With me in the vehicle will be two M-16s and a SAW machine gun. As I explained in an earlier letter, I am a noncombatant and therefore do not carry or fire a weapon. The guidelines for this practice have been established by the Geneva Convention in 1949. However, I will be taken care of very well by my three fellow soldiers (SSG Green, my chaplain assistant, CPT Kennedy, our company commander, and SFC Burgett, our paramedic).

When our convoy is on the highway, we will be spread out over two miles long. As you can imagine, radio communication is vital for the dissipation of confusion and chaos. Hence why we have been training so arduously as a group before our big movement. God willing, we will arrive at our destination without any difficulty and without any incident of harm. Along the way, we will be staying at various other camps. Our accommodations will be sleeping on the ground around our vehicles. And the coolest thing of all is that God wanted me to experience this adventure! (I say this with a bit of nervous laughter) I am not living in fear of what may or may not happen; God has been gracious enough to have given me a peace about what lies ahead. We know our lives belong to our Lord and Savior. As St.

Paul said, "If we live, we live to the Lord. And if we die, we die to the Lord. So, whether we live or die, we belong to the Lord."

That's enough seriousness for now. From the information that we have just recently received from our "advance party" of soldiers who were able to fly up, they have reported that the camp looks reasonable, only needing some hard work and elbow grease to get it in tip-top shape. Presently, there are only a few hundred soldiers at the camp, but over the next three to five months, we will finally reach our maximum number of a few thousand. Do not be surprised or overly concerned if I am unable to write for next Sunday, December 5, as I will be traveling most of the week prior, and I am unsure how extensive internet capabilities are presently in our camp at Q-West. As soon as I am able, I will continue our correspondence. At our base camp in Iraq, we will only have mail delivery and pickup once a week, so the turnaround time for mail will be less frequent than it had been at Camp Virginia, Kuwait.

Lately, our weather has turned amazingly cool. Highs have been in the low- to mid-eighties, and the lows have been in the low- to mid-fifties. We have had several cloudy, somewhat damp days that seem very familiar like back home in the States. The only adverse weather conditions have been the weekly strong windstorms that blow dust and sand all around. These storms make it difficult to do just about anything outside, including driving. There is no reprieve from the dust inside our tents either, since the dust is almost as fine as flour, creeping in and covering everything in the tent. However, this type of weather activity is just a part of living in this country and region. God's people have been doing it here for thousands of years, so I am sure we can make it work also!

I am off to the chow hall for breakfast. We have had about three thousand more soldiers arrive in the last several days, making this place very, very crowded with long lines to get any food, PX items, or go to the MWR tent (like a commons area at college). These all serve as constant reminders that our expectant move to our own piece of turf and work area cannot come soon enough.

We have found out that at our new location we will finally cease living in tents and will have large metal boxes or containers in which to hang our hats. The approximate size for a room will be about eight feet by ten feet and will resemble half of a shipping container. In addition, we will have flushable toilets to use rather than the "porta-potties" that have been our mainstay since our arrival in country. It's the simple things that bring such pleasure!

They are pulling out all the stops for the main meal on Thanksgiving Day for the entire camp. The meal will have the main courses of turkey, roast beef, and lamb with all the trimmings, and they are planning it so that each unit will eat at a designated time in order to allow unit cohesion during this special time. The company commander, the first sergeant, and I will be serving in the chow hall during our unit's eating time. What a great honor and what a good time to see all my soldiers. The next day while y'all are shopping, the camp here will be hosting a 5k fun run called the Turkey Trot. Many of my soldiers will be running together with me for fun. Then we will have to finalize our packing arrangements for the trip north.

Please, continue with your faithful prayers for us as we travel and for more opportunities to proclaim the good news of salvation through Christ. Last Sunday, after our convoy training, we stopped in the middle of the desert, circled the vehicles up, and I held a short service for the group. Obviously, it was not mandatory, but where else could they go? I preached on Jonah and his mission to Nineveh, which is the same area into which we will be traveling. Following the service, our colonel took the opportunity to address the group with encouragement and praise. I surely appreciate his leadership and strength, as do the troops.

Love, Your Pastor

Author's note: My courage faltered as I pondered the dangerous journey north, and I attempted to be honest and yet downplay the risks as I wrote to my flock and to my family. I am the one the troops and even my commander looks to for strength and guidance (sometimes even good luck, like a lucky rabbit's foot on a chain). I am also a husband and a father and a son.

I prayed for a quiet, trusting heart and for our safety. I also shared some of my fears with Carla before we departed, and she comforted me with her words of love and faith. She knew the dangers we faced during this particular convoy and joined me in fervent prayer. I'm thankful I can share these concerns with her. Though perhaps it may seem unfair to burden her with my fears, she is the one I have always trusted to have my back, understand my weaknesses, and share my worries.

My dear love, Carla,

By God's grace, we made it! We are all safe and sound. Praise God. Wow! What an adventure. The surrounding landscape and the incessant wind remind me of the sandhills of western Nebraska where your folks live. I will not be able to call you for some time, as the phone service is very hit and miss. I will email you a detailed letter soon. I LOVE YOU AND MISS YOU. I have your picture up already, along with the candy pop ring and proposal note beside it!

Please give our kids an extra tight hug tonight. I love and miss them so much.

You are my precious gift, your Mark

To my dear parish family,

"The stars at night are big and bright (clap, clap, clap, clap) deep in the heart of Iraq!" Not quite the same song as "Deep in the Heart of Texas," but it does apply here quite nicely. The major reason for such a beautiful expanse of stars upon which to gaze is that we have neither "yard" lights nor streetlights as we did in Kuwait at Camp Virginia. The other reason is that the sky here is just different than in Kuwait. I know how vague this sounds, but it is much the same in the States when one compares the sky in the humid southeast as opposed to the drier southwest. In addition, we have also had some spectacular sunsets and sunrises that would compare with the ones back home at this time of year. So, as you can see, we have all arrived safely here in our new home for the next year, known as Q-West or FOB (Forward Operating Base) Endurance.

We left Camp Virginia on a Sunday; in fact, it was the first Sunday in Advent. Quite apropos since in addition to our journey of preparation for the birth of our Lord, we, as soldiers, were also beginning our journey to our new home, a pilgrimage of sorts. I preached upon the message of John the Baptist, noting his point of "making straight paths in the wilderness," as well as his lifestyle in the wilderness as he prepared his hearers to receive the coming Christ. With that service completed, we mounted up in our vehicles and headed out to our first stop at the Iraq-Kuwait border.

Here, we married up to our five-vehicle escort of the unit we are replacing that had come down from Q-West in order to accompany us on our trek northward, making our convoy nearly thirty vehicles long in number and probably spread out over the highway approximately three miles long. Our sleeping arrangements for our adventure were provided by our vehicles or upon the ground immediately near the vehicles. Being located in the midst of large staging yards for convoys made our place of repose a safe area but very noisy during the wee hours of the morning. Thankfully, our new sleeping bag system provided by the army works quite well in the freezing to subfreezing temperatures that we are experiencing. My place of rest was upon the engine bonnet of our vehicle. Each morning we were up in the darkness and the cold, binding everything together and to our vehicle in preparation for the day's travel.

With the road systems in Iraq being very inconsistent in quality at times, we were often crossing the median of a four-lane road to avoid problem areas. The attendant problems in accomplishing such a maneuver at forty-five to fifty-five mph is obvious; however, when a sandpile just happens to be located near the "crossover," it can get quite dicey in the dark. All of us were able to slide around the mass except for one vehicle whose reaction time was just a bit too slow. After quickly recovering his vehicle— without any damage, I might add—we were on our way again in a matter of minutes. Our first scheduled stop was in the heart of the biblical and historical region known as Ur of the Chaldees. Ending up at a camp on the southern edge of the region around Baghdad left us very tired and ready for a hot meal, a hot shower, and a warm place to sleep. Two out of the three was not bad, with only the warm place to sleep being left out.

In order to get to a major camp on the northeastern edge of the Baghdad region, we took a very "roundabout" route so as to avoid any hotspots. We did have to stop for two IEDs to be removed from the roadway so that we could safely continue on our trip. Crossing the Euphrates River on a pontoon boat left a big impression upon us all, but even more was the beautiful vineyards in and around this bridge. The potential for agriculture in this fertile land is amazing, but the technology and the infrastructure to make it profitable for the average farmer is beyond his reach. Saddam was very cruel in controlling so much of the country's natural resources, rewarding his dishonest cronies and binding the honest workers and farmers.

Our arrival at our new home was greeted with an enthusiasm of permanency. Here, we would make it work for our next eleven months. Our sleeping quarters are as I described previously. How nice not to have sand and dust blow into our stuff and how nice to no longer live out of our rucksacks. I have a real mattress upon which to sleep using my sheet and quilt that I brought with me from home. Every evening our "artillery boys" fire off some illumination rounds. Boy, are they ever loud, and boy, do they ever shake the ground. However, it is a better sound to our ears than if it were from incoming rounds. We are far from the nearest road, and there is no cover under which the bad guys could hide in order even to get close to our compound. In addition, we have Apache helicopters pulling day and night security in and around our camp.

With the increased danger here comes better amenities. The chow hall is the <u>best</u> I have ever eaten. The gym is phenomenal, and it even has a full-sized basketball court, all indoors. The negatives are: poor phone service and wearing our Kevlar helmets all the time. But, really, it isn't as bad as it could be. There are a lot of possibilities here at our camp for future expansions and improvements. Regarding my job, the best part is that I now can do chaplain activities all the time.

I must be making some inroads with my soldiers due to an interesting comment made to me by a few of them. They have often spoken to me about their crude and coarse language and how they are trying to stop. Well, it so happens that when they play Spades and they cuss around one another, they now make each other do five push-ups as punishment for not choosing better words. And like little children confessing to their daddy, they laughingly told me of how many push-ups they have been doing lately during their heated games of Spades. Also, there have been several new faces in our services that weren't there before. It all just takes time, prayers, and patience. God, the Holy Spirit, will work when and where He pleases through the preached Word and through the Sacrament. What a comfort to only be the vessel and not its contents.

Presently, our unit is in the transition mode of operation with our sister CSG who will be leaving in about ten days or so. Interestingly, the chaplain from that unit that I am replacing here went to the Chaplain Advance Course with me back in 2001. After my unit has renovated another building, I will finally have a permanent chapel out of which to operate. Until then, I will be utilizing an area in the MWR (Morale, Welfare, and Recreation) building. So on Sunday mornings, the nonparticipants who just happen to be in and around the building will be hearing us sing hymns and praying prayers.

Singing our Advent hymns this year has struck me in a way that was unexpected. Deeper and broader have the words to these hymns become: "Savior of the Nations, Come," "Hark! A Thrilling Voice is Sounding," "O Lord, How Shall I Meet You," and "Comfort, Comfort, These My People." Given the nature of our needs here, we have broken the tradition of waiting until Christmas to sing Christmas hymns. How powerful hymns are to me! I am so thankful to our God for the gift of song and especially for my church's love to sing these hymns.

Finally, there is a great need here in Iraq for your help. Supplies that are unavailable to the local Iraqi and Kurdish people can be shipped to me for distribution to them through the civil affairs detachment, which regularly visits these villages. The items that are needed can be found anywhere in the States but are either frivolous or unavailable here. Secondly, there are also many items that can be sent to bless the many soldiers with whom I serve. Therefore, I have compiled two lists for you to consider. All the items need to be sealed in plastic bags for their protection and packed thoroughly in boxes. Finally, the boxes should be sealed well with packing tape to insure their stability in handling and in traveling.

For the Iraqi and Kurdish People:

NO RELIGIOUS ARTICLES AT ALL *(This is a humanitarian mission through our government)*

Toiletries of all kinds:
    (for the girls and the ladies: brushes, barrettes, "scrunchies,"
    nail polish, perfume, and basically anything that you, as a
    woman, would appreciate.)

    (for the boys and the men: razors, shaving cream, cologne, and basically anything that you, as a man, would
    appreciate.)

Medical and Health Supplies of all kinds:

Clothing and Shoes:
> (all clothing, for all ages and sexes, should be very modest
> and in good condition)

Toys:
> (Beanie Babies, stuffed animals, trucks, cars, balls—espe-
> cially soccer balls)

For Our Soldiers:

**RELIGIOUS ARTICLES ARE APPRECIATED AND ENCOURAG-
ED** *(This is an evangelistic opportunity. Mark the good as having come from
your parish or your school so that they know we, as Lutherans, love our soldiers
and support them)*

Right now any type of chocolate is priceless:
> (because by March it will be getting too warm for it to be
> shipped over here.)

Microwave popcorn, cookies, nuts, candy, beef jerky and almost any kind
of snack stuff.

Same as above for toiletries, including socks; but no need for medical and
health supplies.

PHOTOS

Easter Sunday Baptism

SERVICES IN THE DESERT

Sandstorm Caused by Shamal Winds

KURDISH SCHOOL CHILDREN

41

Kurdish Women and Children

CHAPLAIN NUCKOLS INVITED TO "PINKIE DANCE" WITH
KURDISH MEN DURING A WEDDING CELEBRATION

KURDISH ELDER

"Biggest Yellow Ribbon in Texas" Wrapped Around the Bell Tower of Saint Paul Lutheran Church Welcoming Chaplain Nuckols Home

The Nuckols Family (Mark, Carla, Mariel, and Patrick)

My dear parish family,

Porcupines in Iraq! Yes, you heard it here first that there are porcupines in Iraq. With no streetlights or yard lights around, we must maneuver to the dining facility, the gym, etc., by flashlight. Last Saturday evening, I see this large form in front of me, lumbering along, and I am thinking to myself, "Is that a soldier low-crawling out here in the middle of nowhere?" As I get closer, the large form in front of me breaks in two, and much to my surprise, I see two large porcupines in my flashlight beam. Isn't it crazy that I have to go to Iraq to see a porcupine in the wild? Well, needless to say, I gave these two friends a wide berth and went on my way quickly. Wow, was my adrenaline ever rushing. I never realized how large porcupines are!

That is one of the most surprising things about this place that I call home for now: the wildlife that roams in the midst of a mostly dry and dusty war zone. Nearby my sleep area there is a little grassy, overgrown patch about the size of the front yard at St. Paul, and in that little patch live four black partridges, complete with their respective brood of chicks. I ran into these birds one morning on my way to my office. Yes, it startled me, and I jumped even though I heard that familiar game bird flapping of wings. No, I can't shoot them, but boy, wouldn't that make quite the hunting story, shooting partridges for Christmas dinner in Iraq!

I must tell you of some tragic news here at Q-West. There was a memorial ceremony conducted last week for two pilots who were recently killed at a nearby base in Mosul. With both being stationed here at Q-West, it will be this base's first memorial ceremony. I met with their chaplain the day after, and he was hurting for his unit and for the pilots' families. Shared suffering binds people together in a very powerful manner. One of the pilots was a young, unmarried lieutenant, and the other was a father of five with the youngest of his children being just ten months old. Due to mechanical problems or due to damage from small arms fire, these pilots somehow lost control of their Apache helicopter while landing, catching the rotor blades of a fully loaded Blackhawk helicopter nearby. Immediately after the soldiers of the Blackhawk disembarked, scrambling off as fast as they were able, both birds burst into flames. Only the pilots of the Apache were killed. All of the fifteen occupants of the Blackhawk were only shook up but not injured, thanks be to God. However, two of our soldiers were on this helicopter. Their belongings were all burned up, but they were all safe and sound. They both will be returning soon. I will be talking to them and checking on them. Interestingly, this tragedy occurred at the same place into which I flew just last week.

Are we not in God's hands? Absolutely, we are! He will see my unit and me through all things, including events such as this. Sadly but realistically, there will probably be more such events while I am serving here. Join me in praying for these pilots' families and for their unit, which has only been here in country just two months, still having ten more to go.

Now, on to more joyful matters. My group of soldiers who have been gathering for Sunday services these last couple of months are becoming more "Lutheran" every Sunday. They have told me how much they appreciate the explanations of spiritual matters found in the catechism. Most of them had never heard of the catechism, but in our little Armed Forces Devotional Book put out by our church, therein it is contained. I have used it for our edification at our services with the Ten Commandments, the Creed, and will soon use it with the Lord's Prayer.

Therefore, while I am here with these sheep given to me, under these circumstances, there is gathered together a group of Christians who are faithfully confessing the biblical faith as we become a small battleground congregation. Of course, they may return to their respective churches or choose not to attend anywhere upon completion of our deployment. However, these fellow believers whom we will see in heaven will have heard and have been *comforted* by the church's teachings, which we are professing and which are the confessions of the one true faith. About the Lord's faithfully preached word did Isaiah the prophet proclaim, "...so shall my word be that goes out from my mouth; it shall not return to me empty, but it shall accomplish that which I purpose, and shall succeed in the thing for which I sent it" (Is. 55:11). Or as is sung in a great hymn by Martin Franzmann, "The sower sows; his reckless love scatters abroad the goodly seed, intent alone that men may have the wholesome loaves that all men need. Though some be snatched, and some be scorched, and some be choked and matted flat, the sower sows; his heart cries out, 'Oh what of that, and what of that?' Preach you the Word and plant it home, and never faint; the Harvest Lord who gave the sower seed to sow will watch and tend His planted Word" (*LW* 259). This experience is giving me new insight into missions and evangelical matters.

We, as Christians, do not need to "water down" nor "make more manageable" the one true faith of the one holy, catholic, and apostolic church, which we proclaim and confess. Through our confessing this faith clearly and confessing this faith often, the Holy Spirit will do the rest through His means of salvation, he properly preached Word, and the rightly administered Sacraments. These theological terms, which are sometimes abstract, find their concretization when faithfully put into practice. Brothers and sisters, the harvest is ripe: pray to the Lord of the harvest to send out workers into His harvest field. To God alone be the glory.

Love, Your Pastor

My dear parish family,

Damp, dreary, rainy weather brought us Christmas Eve and Christmas Day; however, with the threat level of an attack by the insurgents at a very high state, the weather acted more like a friend sent from God, impeding any attack upon us over the holy days. We had been given an abundance of intelligence pointing to a follow-up attack similar to the one that occurred in the dining facility at Camp Marez in Mosul. Nevertheless, we were not thwarted in our celebration of the holy birth of Christ. Beginning with a well-attended service of lessons and carols, we sang our way into the joy that accompanies the saving faith in Immanuel born for us.

We were comforted by God's promises during a time full of mixed emotions and distant thoughts. It was so very good to see some of the more "hardened" soldiers stop by to worship who have never attended before. God has His way with us and uses our feeble attempts to reach out to others; thanks be to God for such grace to be used by Him. Afterward we shared goodies from our care packages, along with some yummy finger food from our dining facility. Our colonel gladly delivered Christmas "care packages," playing up the role as Santa with his soldiers, which brought many smiles and laughter. As a whole, the evening seemed surreal since we were singing all of the right songs, hearing all of the right messages, seeing all of the right trimmings, but not doing any of these familiar rituals with our loved ones in a known setting. Therefore, it will be a Christmas that none of us will ever forget due to the unusual circumstances under which it was celebrated. Later that evening, the faithful few Lutherans remained for the midnight Mass celebrating the gift that Christ has given unto His bride, the church, to sustain her in her pilgrimage, and we were richly sustained by the bread from heaven.

Christmas Day was celebrated at the dining facility with the pomp and circumstance that can be done in a place like this with the only resources that are available. For example, the workers constructed large Christmas tree-type structures with pop cans and coffee cans. They were garnished with the obligatory blinking lights and with nonobligatory spray-painted doughnuts and breads; I guess you would have to see it to believe it. We had wonderful food upon which to sup and beautiful displays upon which to feast our eyes that were carved in melons and decorated upon cakes. Conversations around the tables were mostly about our families, about what they were doing, and about what traditions we practiced at this holy time of the year. It was enjoyable, but it was without our families. Needless to say, the value of having family and enjoying their presence has risen to a height unequaled heretofore; they are a gift from our loving Father and are cherished as such.

Pastors around the world have known for years that the Sunday following Christmas always tends to be one with very low attendance. However, God has a way of doing things that continually leaves us mystified. Presently, I host a Sunday morning Protestant service in the movie room at our MWR building. Well, last Sunday morning there was a miscommunication by the director of the facility, and we were preempted by a major meeting of the Iraqi leaders from the local villages in and around our base. The MWR director apologized all over himself, asking if we would be willing to have our service in the computer lab/reading room. Somewhat slighted by their mistake, I moved our larger than normal group of soldiers into the new venue. There, in that room, God had miraculously allowed us to be in the presence of about thirty more soldiers who were at the various computer stations. While we sang Christmas hymns, read the Scriptures, and prayed to our loving Father, these thirty extra "worshippers" also heard the message of Christ's love for us as sinners in these hymns, in the readings, in the sermon, and in the prayers. I could have never planned a better evangelistic/outreach event if I had tried. And, in addition, I normally would never have been allowed to hold such a service in that room while others were using it, since they might have been offended by our presence.

God sure can allow a great opportunity to occur, and all we do is just blindly fall into it; to God alone be the praise and the glory!

We are the main handler of all goods coming in from Turkey, and we work closely with the truck drivers who bring these goods into Iraq from Turkey, not only to supply our army but also to supply the people of Iraq. Interestingly, these Turkish truck drivers are not a part of any major Turkish trucking firm as we are so accustomed to seeing in the USA. Instead, they are all independent drivers who operate their own rigs. Allow me to explain this even further. Many small villages pool their monies in order to purchase a rig, which is then driven by a volunteer from that same village, and all this is done in order to help bring money into their impoverished lives. You see, these drivers are able to make two to three times what they could make in Turkey, thus making the risk worth it for themselves and for their villages, so to speak.

Gun trucks from our base escort them from the Turkish border; then we hand them off to be escorted by gun trucks from a base further south in order to complete their journey all the way to Baghdad. Once the loads arrive in Baghdad, local Iraqi drivers take these loads and distribute them throughout the nation. Sadly, the "bad guys" here have decided to specifically pick on these Turkish truck drivers by repeatedly attacking their convoys so as to break their will in assisting us and the Iraqi people. As you can imagine, when there are casualties, the loss is great; an extended family/village has lost all their investment, both financially and humanly. I realize that this type of existence has always occurred around the world at various times and places, but as in all things, I have realized it more clearly by working with it so closely. For you see, when the drivers are killed, we also handle their remains, escorting them back to the Turkish border, where oftentimes the family has borrowed some sort of transportation in order to pick up their loved ones. Here, as in most of the world, the family has intimate connection with their dead, physically handling their loved one's body and, ultimately, laying it to rest in the ground.

On to a more pleasant subject: my family and their Christmas wonderings. They were able to spend a week at Carla's parents' and enjoy the time away from school and the routine in Kansas City. While in Nebraska, they shared with me how small our world really is. My father-in-law, as many of you know, is a retired pastor who has served various vacancies in and around the North Platte area. Recently, he has been assisting at a small parish in a town about seventy miles southeast of North Platte. It just so happens in that parish is a woman whose brother is my chaplain assistant. So when my father-in-law shared one of my letters with the parish, this woman asked him more detailed questions about me and my location. They both were in awe when they came to realize that they were talking about the same people. By the way, my chaplain assistant is not Lutheran, nor is any of his family except this sister who joined the church when she married. I share this story with you to let you know how our lives affect other people of whom we are rarely aware.

Allow me to tell you one more similar story regarding this same point. When I was on active duty at Fort Campbell, Carla worked with a retired colonel at the local Red Cross message center. He always had a soft spot for her and for me because his recently deceased wife was brought up Lutheran. He is now in his mid- eighties and is faithful in corresponding at Christmas. Carla had mentioned to him in our Christmas letter that I had been deployed. He, in turn, told his daughter who, as you can imagine, is an avid supporter of our troops. Recently, I received a letter of encouragement from her with a vow to pray for us and a commitment to send some "care packages" for my soldiers. The ultimate application of these musings is the sharing of our faith and the Lord's work in our dust-filled lives. His message of salvation and His works of love through us get around even though we do not realize it! Never cease to share the hope of salvation and the kind deeds of the forgiven life that you have been given because the repercussions of such feeble sharings are profound and will leave us speechless on the day of our entrance into heaven when our Lord will say, "Well done, good and faithful servants."

Love, Pastor

My dear friends and family,

How gracious you all have been in sending me and my soldiers such wonderful cards and such yummy goodies to share; thank you so very much! Personally speaking, your sweet and loving words to me have meant so very much. We all need to know that we are loved and remembered, and I thank you for doing so to me. Everyone here in the 917th has heard of the chaplain's "fan club," those loving Lutherans back in the States! Thankfully, y'all don't send me any lutefisk, uffdah! My soldiers have heard me speak often and at length about my parishes and their kindnesses. You have made a big impact upon these men and women. Most of the boxes that you have sent take about two to four weeks to arrive, so pack them well, tape them up well, and keep them coming! Thank you again for this amazing kindness!

This region of Iraq used to be known as Assyria, and ever since Christianity arrived here in the second century AD, the church has always had a presence here in spite of the many and tumultuous power struggles over the centuries. In recent years, there has been an increase of violence against these, our fellow saints in Christ. Their churches have been bombed and vandalized, their lives have been threatened and ended, yet they have not stopped gathering for the Supper, nor have they ceased in their outreach by word and by deed. So markedly different is their existence than ours that it bears investigation. These men and women do not concern themselves with proving their right to exist, nor do they concern themselves with proving the success of their message. Instead, they concern themselves with matters more important and profound, gathering as a body of Christ in a world that despises such gatherings and faithfully reaching out in word and deed to all their neighbors. Herein lies the format for our evangelism program that has its roots in the early church and has survived for years preaching Christ crucified in a hostile environment, concerned only with fidelity to the One who has called them by the gospel, enlightened with His gifts, sanctified and keeps them in the one true faith. Whenever you pray the Lord's Prayer, you are praying for these brothers and sisters in the faith, for the kingdom of God has come and is still coming even during the upheaval in the Iraqi nation. How comforting for us and them to know the timelessness of our message and the blessed hope of the resurrection!

Last week we had a traumatic event occur in the middle of the night when a special ops C-130 crash-landed on our airstrip. It had just landed when the pilot undershot a bomb crater and instead plowed into it, jamming the front landing gear through the fuselage and belly skidding to a halt. By God's grace, none of the crew or the passengers, including a chaplain and his assistant, were killed. Several were injured and had to be med-evacuated, but all were alive! I was very proud of our medical personnel and our combat lifesavers who assisted, proving that our frequent training is beneficial. The only humorous note affiliated with this accident occurred a few days later when they destroyed the remains of the aircraft. The explosion came during our New Year's Day dinner while we sat unaware and shook the building tremendously, leaving everyone scampering about thinking that we were under attack. You can imagine the nervous laughter and chatter that followed our realization of what really happened. The adrenaline rush subsided when we realized we were safe.

Finally, a pastoral exhortation. Get out that catechism while studying your Bibles and review the profound Scriptural truths contained therein, for they still have application to us and to our faith even though it may have been years since we were confirmed. Here's an example of why. The last couple of Sundays I have been using the section on the Lord's Prayer and its meaning in our Sunday services. Most of the soldiers have never seen or heard of such a document but were so very thankful and vocal about the concise and substantive explanation with which we are so familiar. Luther was right when he said that the one who masters the catechism really ought to be called a Doctor of Theology. Our Lord said it better when

He proclaimed, "If you abide in My word, you are truly My disciples, and you will know the truth, and the truth will set you free" (John 8:31–32).

Love, Pastor

My dear parish family,

The skies have opened here with rain, more rain, and even a little more rain on top of it all. The annual amount for this area of Iraq is around eleven to twelve inches, and if my little homemade rain gauge is correct, I believe we have received a third of that over the last four days. Drainage here is a problem and the soil not very conducive in absorbing rain in general. Then throw in a high volume of large truck traffic, and voila, we have the makings of a great SUV commercial spot! Seriously, the men and women who faithfully drive these transportation convoys in this weather and, for that matter, in any weather, with all sorts of supplies, are doing a fantastic job. Several of our subordinate units are delivering the ballots for the upcoming election as well as providing other necessary supplies up here in the Mosul area. Many of these brave Americans who are not even twenty-five years old are being entrusted with a rig and with a load in excess of what most of them will earn in ten years. They have made a difference for this nation's birth of freedom and will continue assisting them as long as they are here.

It is a privilege to be here at this time, and in this place, in order to assist these people in the establishment of a democracy, albeit an infantile one. During the two days prior to election and one day after Election Day, our dining facility will be only serving breakfast and midnight short order. Safety here is not so much the reason for the change but rather the supplies will not be available during those days, since all convoy movements of any type will not be allowed on the roads anywhere in country those days. How quickly we can get used to such little things as three hot-cooked meals, yet all of this is about protecting our soldiers during what is expected to be above normal attacks by the insurgents. Keep this and all that follows in your prayers, thank you.

After the crash of the C-130 cargo plane due to a major bomb crater in the runway, we have accomplished the repair of the airstrip here, and air operations have begun again in earnest. What an experience it has been to see and to hear several of these and other types of cargo aircraft regularly land and take off here. With the advent of these flights, we now have a detachment of airmen from the air force to coordinate and handle the aircraft. Amazing, indeed, is the amount of supplies that can be loaded onto these aircraft. In the near future, we will be receiving cargo flights directly from the States in addition to these intra-theater supply flights.

Carla has put our home on the market, which will make my return to the States and our homecoming to Austin happen more easily. We both would like to find something close to the church but are aware of the recent spike in property values. She and the kids have really worked hard getting our yard back into shape in order to sell since the last time when we attempted the same. The tornado that hit the neighborhood last year has made selling a little more complicated. The brand-new homes rebuilt just a block to our north are certainly drawing those looking to buy. All in God's time!

The ice storms that have plagued the Midwest have had their way with several of our trees, leaving them somewhat unshapely, but they will bounce back in the spring. You men must know how helpless I feel being here in Iraq and unable to take care of these matters for her and for our family, but God has seen fit to have blessed us with a strappin' young man named Patrick and a friend of his, Chad, who help her out with some of the more physical chores. I keep telling him that his mom is helping him with his weightlifting program by allowing him to pitch in. He gladly does these things for her and is paid handsomely in pints of ice cream of his choosing! Mariel is our organizer and can spiff up any room in a matter of minutes! She appreciates car keys over ice cream!

Basketball games have resumed following Christmas break with plenty of action to keep Carla on the road carting the kids and friends over an hour's drive for most of the away games. Thankfully, both kids play at the same court on the same night. Patrick is playing both junior varsity and varsity level, enjoying himself and scoring several points at the same time. I am getting tired thinking about how he will "school" me with his prowess when I return. Oh well, being humbled is a good thing, right?

Mariel entered this, her last basketball season, with some ambivalence toward the game but has grown in her enjoyment as her skills have improved. She accomplished a "double-double" the other evening. A double-double is when a player has double digits in scoring and in rebounding. I have been teasing her about her lack of desire for the game before the season and how her recent stats don't seem to show such apathy! Last weekend, both kids had a great time celebrating their high school's winter homecoming. My sweetie is very busy with our kids' schedules, as you can see. What a blessing to have been given a marriage to such a woman and to have the joy of our children. To God be the glory.

Love, Pastor Nuckols

My dear parish family,

Consider the relative peacefulness that accompanies the democratic process in our nation. Consider also the calmness with which we have an exchange of political power in our nation where a plethora of various conflicting ideologies exist. In the United States, voter turnout for the various local, state, and national elections tends to be quite low, even though there is no bombing at the polling places or any threats against our families. Now, consider the voter turnout at the recent Iraqi election where the safety of the voter and his/her family was in question. Let us never forget the price of our own freedom as well as the contempt that is often shown it by our apathy at the various elections. Being present during this historic event adds to my convictions of the great civic responsibility that we all bear to be involved in our own nation's political process. Truly, we are a blessed people who sometimes forget the obligation that we bear in order to maintain such freedoms and such peace within our borders.

With the Iraqi elections going so well, there has been an increase in the confidence of the average Iraqi toward this political process. We have had a sharp increase in the passing of information regarding the identity of the insurgents and the locations of their whereabouts as well as their weapons' whereabouts. Prior to the elections, the locals were much less revealing of information concerning their enemies. But after thirty-five years of oppression, the Shia Muslims have been given a voice in the democratic process. And in this region of Iraq, the northern quarter, the minority Kurdish population who have been oppressed and abused now have a larger voice in their welfare.

Today, following my worship services for Transfiguration Sunday, I will be heading further north and west to the Turkish-Iraqi border. We have a small contingent of soldiers there who have not had a chaplain come for about a month. These men and women oversee the vital inflow of supplies, especially fuel from Turkey. In traveling northward, we must go through some snow-covered mountain passes in order to arrive at this small outpost that sits at the foot of many more snow-covered peaks. We will be delivering their mail, some supplies that they are without, and I will be doing some counseling as well as bringing them the Word of God in some worship services. This trip had been planned earlier, but due to the cessation of all traffic on the roads with the elections, we have had to postpone it.

Presently, I have three soldiers who are taking catechetical instruction. One has very little church background and the other two have a very broad church experience, yet without any biblical substance. The common thread that all three of these men have is a basic desire to systematically study the content of the historic confession of the Christian faith. Their words to me have been very revealing as to the current crisis within American Christendom, which is a lack of substance in the preaching, in the teaching, and in the worship found in some churches that are more concerned with only a social message. Indeed, I observed this almost ten years ago by the same age group of soldiers while I served on active duty at the 101st Airborne Division. The desire for a concise, substantial confession of the Christian faith was also what attracted me to Luther's Small Catechism, which is nothing more than a terse proclamation of the one holy, Christian, and apostolic faith revealed in Scripture alone, received by faith alone, and built upon Christ alone.

I just received an email from my kids, which stated that BOTH of them will be in the spring play at Lutheran High. They haven't performed together on the same stage since Mrs. Meier's musicals back at Holy Cross when they were in grade school. I am looking forward to the DVD that they promised to send me of this comedy. Is our house big enough for two stars? Only their mother can keep them humble enough to coexist in the same abode!

Your prayers and your encouragement have been vital in sustaining my morale and that of my family, thank you! What a blessing God worked in my life on that March day when He marked me His own and placed His seal of salvation upon me through my baptism. He grafted me into the communion of saints, giving me a loving family from which I will never be parted.

Love, Pastor

My dear friends,

Allow me to share with you some fascinating history regarding an area of present-day Iraq and regarding a people often forgotten by the world who have been sorely oppressed and brutally mishandled. The entire northern fourth of Iraq is inhabited by a distinct culture known as the Kurdish people. Within this unique culture are Muslims as well as Christians, who have peacefully coexisted together for over a thousand years. When Saddam Hussein came into his corrupt power, it was very beneficial for him to work out trade agreements with the Turks. However, for him to do so meant that he would bypass the sovereignty of the Kurdish people as a distinct sub-nation. Equally beneficial for Hussein to do was to take over a rich oil-producing Kurdish city and area. In doing so, he murdered thousands upon thousands of innocent Kurdish men, women, and children in a holocaust of sorts. Driving them away from their cities of commerce and from their fields, he also inflicted horrible economic suffering. In addition, Saddam surgically removed over four hundred whole villages by annihilating them through horrendous means or simply by displacing them. Sadly, as these Kurdish refugees fled toward Turkey, the Turks slaughtered them at the border. Suffice to say, because they were not an internationally recognized nation, the world threw up its hands in supposed helplessness while Saddam continued his atrocities.

Now, because of our involvement here in Iraq, the Kurdish people will have a large voice in the forming of this new democratic Iraqi nation. This Kurdish region is the only part of Iraq that shares its border with Turkey. And due to the violence against the Kurds, there is not a very positive relationship between the Turks and the Kurds. Though I don't mean to be overly simplistic in this analysis, we have become a buffer for the political and economic future of the Kurds and, for that matter, the Iraqi nation as it assimilates again as a formerly disenfranchised people.

Having traveled up north with my colonel and command sergeant major, we accomplished quite a bit visiting and rapport building with the local nationals in the short days we spent there. There were several important meetings with the local dignitaries and the local power brokers who run the shipping industry here at the border. We met with THE general over the entire Kurdish region of Iraq, having the obligatory hot, sweet tea with him, his police chief, and the commander of his special forces. Following our hour-long conversation through two translators, we were treated with a traditional Kurdish meal and discussed the two topics that could be the most inflammatory, politics and religion. The interchange between my colonel and the general was very beneficial for building a relationship of trust. It was a great honor, indeed, to be invited by my command to attend such a high-level meeting. Fascinating would be the most appropriate word to describe the afternoon's conversations and meetings.

Thinking that I had witnessed several great events, I found these were to be topped by a much less formal conversation with a soldier following my evening worship service. A loving friend of this young man had been speaking with him, at length, about the Christian faith and thus, causing the young man to be assured that he was a believer, or if not, what did he have to do in order to become a believer. We talked, searched the Scriptures, and prayed for over three hours. Following this fruitful interchange, he asked about being baptized. After several more hours of catechesis regarding baptism, I baptized him at the unit's first-aid clinic here at Habur Gate, Iraq.

I was also privileged to be used in a young woman's life. She was the medic that had patched up several bloodied soldiers who had been ambushed while they were on a convoy mission. She still has nightmares regarding this incident, and no one here can relate since none have seen or have experienced such a firefight. How humbling it was for me to be used by God in these young people's spiritual lives to be trusted with their emotions, their fears, and their trials. I am only beginning to understand what the circuit riders of the past must have gone through with their infrequent visits to the remote groups of believers that they served. I will be frequenting this outpost at least once a month since they are needful of chaplain support much more than I had imagined.

On our final day we met with the governor of a province in Turkey. He was inquiring about the remains of three Turkish truck drivers who were killed immediately outside our base in early December of last year. Thankfully it hasn't turned into a political fiasco yet, but as to why there has been over sixty days passed since their deaths without the release of the bodies is a mystery. My colonel said he will personally handle this issue and will personally deliver the bodies. The governor was very pleased with the colonel's interest in solving this issue. I am sure that the governor will be returning the favor in a manner that will benefit the truck traffic here in northern Iraq. It seems that this is the way things work in this culture—a scratching of each other's backs.

Having made several connections with the translators that are being utilized by our troops, upon my return trips, I will be utilizing these translators in the distribution of the supplies to these Kurdish villagers, which have been lovingly sent. In addition, I will be sending you pictures of them when they receive your kind gifts. I think you'll be really pleased to see what your help will do for these children and families. The terrain here is very rugged and mountainous, and the winters are very wet and cold with many of the children running around barefooted or in sandals. With your help, many of the kiddos will have shoes or boots for the coming cold.

Regarding one of the Turkish translators who spoke with me at length about Christianity, about who Jesus is, and about the authorship of the Scriptures following our long conversation, he gave me his email and asked when I would return in order to continue our conversation about these spiritual matters. God uses us where we are. Continue living out your faith, for your heavenly Father will use you just as He has since you became His child.

My Love, Pastor

My dear parish family,

An adventure was had by all. When we left Turkish-Iraqi border around 10 p.m. in the evening, the expectations of easy travel for our return convoy were minimal. Traveling at night allowed us good cover for the nearly one hundred trucks full of fuel and supplies bound for our US forces in northern Iraq. Organizing and directing such a fleet of vehicles driven by non-English-speaking drivers in good weather and in daylight is a challenge indeed. To do the same under the cover of darkness and in freezing mist/rain/fog is THE example of herding cats. With no more than ten miles under our belt of the nearly 175-mile trek, we encountered the problematic weather and slowed to a crawling speed of fifteen mph. Thus began our adventure.

One third of the trucks took a wrong turn, being unable to see the vehicles in front of them, and the other third were stuck behind a truck that had broken down. The snow had accumulated to nearly a foot, and the roads were glass smooth with frozen precipitation. Before describing the "rest of the story," it is essential to add the traffic of oncoming vehicles, driven by local Iraqis and others, had little regard for speed limits or basic road manners. No, there wasn't the familiar sight of salt trucks laying down their blanket of protection from the elements to enable safe travel; there was only the common sense, or the lack thereof, each driver possessed. Unfortunately, nearly all the drivers coming toward us had left that essential ingredient at home when they ventured forth in the wee hours of the morning.

By the time we had finally recovered the lost kittens of our convoy, it was daylight, and we found ourselves in the rough area of the violent city of Mosul. When we stopped to regroup and to await the arrival of the last segment of our procession, nerves were raw from the lack of sleep and from the stress of the previous nine hours of chaos. Not yet near Q-West, our destination and home, we needed to refuel our army vehicles before we completed the final leg of our convoy from hell.

The drivers entrust themselves into the hands of the convoy leaders with no real knowledge of their exact destination, so to allow them to enter the base in Mosul would signify to them their objective had been reached. Now, in order to motivate these exhausted non-English speaking drivers back onto the road in a timely fashion would be more than humanly possible. Therefore, being in the lead vehicle, the colonel and I lined up and corralled this unwieldy snake into somewhat of an organized gaggle so that we could continue on to Q-West following the rapid refuel of our army vehicles. Our "on the spot" creation was aligned immediately outside the front gate of one of our Mosul bases. Boy, did we create a hullabaloo with the traffic jam and such. The only thing that saved us from the curses and the obscene gestures was the fact that the colonel was out there in the midst of all the confusion and bedlam. We had tanks, Stryker vehicles, and other "hard-core trigger-pullers" bypassing to the left and to the right of our stray litter of cats.

Finally, after more than thirteen hours on those treacherous and unforgiving roads, we arrived at our home with sunshine to boot. Drained, numb, and spent are the best adjectives to describe the thirty-three-hour day through which we had been thrust. But what a sense of accomplishment we had been given by the grace of God! What was the hidden blessing in the weather? It kept all of the bad guys home and away from us on those roads. God has a way of providing about which we could never comprehend nor of which we could ever plumb the depths. Beneficial, indeed, was the "firsthand" learning that our colonel received, allowing him to standardize all convoy operations and to enact more safety measures.

Your kind outpouring of goodies and health-care items have begun to arrive. How wonderful! I have enjoyed sharing the edibles with my soldiers and would be remiss if I didn't taste-test them for freshness every day. Because of the great selection of victuals you have sent, I have had a regular stream of soldiers stopping by my office for a "snack break." Usually, they will sit down for a moment and talk with me about the goings-on with their work, their family back home, or some other pertinent matter that concerns their heart. These contributions of yours have allowed doors to be opened with some of these soldiers who wouldn't normally drop by and talk; thank you!

In about three weeks from now, I will be delivering to the Kurds in the northern towns of Habur Gate and Zahko, near the Turkish border, most of the clothing items, toiletries, and other items that you sent for the local population. These highly appreciative people about whom I wrote last week will be so thrilled to see your strong expression of Christian love in the form of these goods. How wonderful for me to be used as your hands in the distribution of these gifts!

Finally, I would like to share with you a brief reflection from my personal journal on God's expectations of me and my expectations of myself. These two rarely are in sync with one another. The application for all Christians is in how God provides us with all that we need to share our faith and proclaim His grace and mercy:

> *They all want something of me when they come to church. They all expect that I have something to give them. A pastor is a man who is beset by the expectation that he has something to give. And when they all expect that you have something to give, you finally get the idea yourself that you have something to give.*

> *Do you really have something to give? God help you never to grow so conscious of your ministerial office or your dignity that as you grow older, more experienced and mature, you come to be convinced in all "humility" that you have something to give!*

> *What can you give to him who has been lying in the same bed for twenty years, paralyzed and shrunken, and yet is friendly, quiet, patient, even joyful in the Lord? What are you going to*

give to the dying young consumptive whose mother has called you to come, and you find him in utter despair? What are you going to give to those people in the pews who have been disciplined in suffering and patience for thirty years and more, much longer than you have? What are you, who are only a man, going to give to men like yourself?

But stop your questions! Tell me, what language are you speaking? Are you speaking the language of the poor in spirit, or are you speaking the language of unbelief? Do you have nothing to give? Don't you have something else to give? Don't you bring with that Book from the pulpit, which is God's treasure for you and people like you? Has not the chalice and the bread been entrusted to you, so that you need not go to the hungering and thirsting with empty hands? Does not God have something to give? And can't you take as much as you need in order to be able to give?

Woe is me. Am I speaking the language of faith, or is it the voice of the Tempter that is whispering to me, "God's gifts are in your hand; just go ahead and use them"? Get thee behind me, Satan! I have nothing to give, but God will give to me and my brethren, as he did yesterday and today, so tomorrow, out of the immeasurable riches of his grace. Amen.

My dear parish family,

A new phase in our deployment has begun. With it brings great joy and with it brings great sorrow. Great sorrow because the inevitability of the return trip is always present, but great joy because of the anticipation of reunion with spouse, children, and a familiar environment. We have already sent four groups of soldiers back to the States for their two-week furlough (R and R, rest and recreation). All of them have returned with enjoyment and relaxation as their main course.

The responsibility of counseling these expectant soldiers regarding all the emotions that they will experience when they return to their loved ones has been given to me. How fortunate am I to have the opportunity to privately speak with every soldier of my unit regarding emotionally intimate matters as well as spiritually intimate matters before they enjoy their respite at home. Such personal time with these men and women has allowed me the honor of being trusted with their concerns and fears, taking them to our Father's throne of grace for His strength and mercy.

Due to being away from the familiarity of our home, new habits and routines mark our daily lives here in this distant land as the days move into weeks and into months. When these new practices of ours come into contact with our homelife, which has grown accustomed to our absence, there will always be times of stress from this, our reintegration. How could such a delightful experience be marked with such emotional complexity? Just as there was a surplus of sensations through which to sort when each of us left the predictability of our daily lives in the States, coming to this very kinetic environment that makes up a battlefield, so also our family members sampled the same cornucopia of moods and feelings with our temporary exodus. For the purpose of my counsel to these soldiers, the army has taught me about this emotional cycle through which we will all travel. However, actually participating in this cycle is quite another learning experience, which transcends all book knowledge with its elucidations of mere charts and graphs.

Some of the soldiers have said that it was harder to leave their loved ones following their furlough than it was when they first come into the Iraqi theater. Others disagree, with the reason being because they know what to expect when they return to their post here in Iraq. Either way, in spite of all of the emotional upheaval, the soldiers have unequivocally found their time with the family to be quite precious and inestimable in value. For that I am very thankful for the army's commitment to the soldier with this furlough program.

In order to offer another off-duty activity that is constructive for the soldier, I have begun teaching basic guitar lessons to a group of four Buddy Holly wannabes. They didn't know that the chaplain cut his proverbial "guitar" teeth on good old '70s rock and roll. We have had a fun time together, and as always, before the lessons are through, the conversation turns to talk about God. These four gentlemen aren't attending any worship service presently, but we'll see about that. (smile)

On the home front, Patrick's basketball team is the undefeated conference champion, which is a first in a long time for Lutheran High of Kansas City. Both kids will be very busy this week with the district playoffs, and Carla's trucking firm will be responsible for the transportation of both children and their "stuff," which accompanies them to every game. Mariel's senior class trip is less than three weeks away. Her class decided upon the Big Apple (New York City) for their destination, and for many of them, it will be their first trip to the east coast and to a very large metropolitan city. Stories will abound like dandelions in an empty field, and I cannot wait to hear of her adventures.

Love, your Pastor

My dear little flock,

The following letter may be difficult to read due to the subject matter, which deals with death. Today I write with a heavy heart. We had two of our soldiers killed in a tragic vehicular accident on their way back to our base. The first soldier was killed instantly, as he was the gunner on the top of the vehicle. The other died about twenty-four hours later from the injuries sustained in the rollover of the vehicle. The company commander of these two soldiers took the news very hard the first time I informed him, but he broke down in my arms when I told him about his second soldier twenty-four hours later. He has a big heart for his soldiers and is a compassionate man. It was his first experience with the death of one of his soldiers in his eighteen years of service, some of it as an NCO and the remainder as an officer.

Of course, the effect of this tragedy upon the unit was substantial. They have known one another for a couple of years already, working closely on various missions with each other. One of the unit's soldiers was especially traumatized by the event. Best friends and roommates describes the soldier's relationship with the two deceased. About an hour was spent in my attempt to soothe the hysteria that had been fed by the severe sorrow and other such emotions. Then, twenty-four hours later, that fresh wound had to be opened again when I announced the second death. My heart was broken in observing the grief and sorrow of these men and women.

While the bodies of these soldiers return to the States for burial, the unit gathers for a memorial ceremony to commemorate their lives and their service. At the front of the theater stood a display with two M-16s affixed with their bayonets being held downward in the stand. On the unfathomable of the weapon is their boots. Sobering, traumatic, and full of emotion would be the most apt words to describe the scene. At this highly traditional ceremony, there is also a twenty-one-gun salute for each of the deceased as well as taps being played. All this regalia is essential in allowing the unit to mourn and to bring closure to an experience that will never be forgotten. Watching these young soldiers forced to grow up quite suddenly and abruptly before my eyes is a sight that I will always carry with me.

Grasping the unfathomable application of God's holy Word in these soldiers' lives is humbling. To realize the immeasurable relevance of these same Scriptures in my life leaves me overwhelmed. Regularly, I read the pericopes of whose substance I am familiar, and yet, now while living in different circumstances, new applications and their attendant benefits are brought by the continual rereading of those same precious, recognizable passages. The verses' direct applications were never hidden, only the eyes of the reader did sin cloud its significance to the present. Thus the timelessness of God's Word and the fruitfulness of God's Word for the lives of His sinner/saints, of which I count myself.

In addition to the death of our precious soldiers, last Sunday (Lent 3) we had our first rocket attack by the insurgents. Quite a bit of ruckus was raised as well as dust and such. No one was injured, thanks be to God. If you hear of anything on the media, we are all safe. This type of attack is very haphazard and highly inaccurate, but with 122 mm rockets, inaccuracy is overcome by their larger payload. The maximum range of these projectiles is approximately 15 km, or about 9.3 miles; these were fired from about six miles out. Our movement unit, the "trigger-pullers," quickly searched the area, finding the launch site but no bad guys. The possibility of a rocket attack has been known for about two weeks, but with the lack of insurgent activity lately, it was thought that our movement unit had already found the cache of weapons and the bad guys too. However, with such an event as this, we are very quickly reminded that we are still very vulnerable.

Your kind outpouring of gifts is to be praised and heartily acknowledged. My soldiers have asked me repeatedly to thank you all for these simple pleasures that you have brought into their lives. Such packages have made me a popular man, as well as an unpopular man. Being popular is not hard if one has chocolate, snacks, and goodies to share, but unpopular because most of the mail has been addressed to me. The picture that you saw last week was of the forty-seven boxes that all arrived on the same day! It has been so much fun to share your goodness with these men and women, thank you for the privilege to do so.

Please keep these dear soldiers and their families in your daily prayers. The pressures they must bear are immeasurable.

My love to you, Pastor

My dear parish family,

While you remembered the great missionary efforts of Ireland's patron saint, St. Patrick, I had traveled up to the Turkish-Iraqi border to visit some of my soldiers, to bring them a service of the Word, and to distribute among the Kurdish villagers some of the aid that you all have so lovingly sent. By the way, Patrick means nobleman!

On the morning of our humanitarian aid mission, we met with the mayor of this region who would be accompanying us as well as eight of his armed policemen. Before we left on this undertaking, his hospitality had to be shown by having us sit down in his office for tea and for conversation. He showed me a document that was signed by Saddam Hussein in 1974 ordering the destruction of Kurdish villages in this region and the murder of their people. Bitterness was neither in his voice nor in his words but rather optimism for the future that our presence here in Iraq has given for his people and for this region's future. He spoke of the overall harmony that exists between the Muslims and the Christians of his region, their unity existing not in religion but in nationality.

With our substantive pleasantries complete and with the sincere ritual of hospitality finished, we began our trek to some rural schools and villages. Their schools were conducted in a very interesting manner, educating them together in broad age groups, somewhat similar to the one-room schoolhouse models of our rural past. Whenever we, as guests, would enter their very simple and sparsely adorned rooms, the entire class stood up and greeted us with a loudly chanted salutation. These nine- to fourteen-year-olds were learning English, Kurdish, and Arabic, their math instruction was prealgebra, and their geography was very thorough, humbling some of my soldiers. Three of the six teachers were especially introduced to me because they are Christians, proudly adorning their persons with the common symbol of our common faith, the cross. Kids are kids and teachers are teachers no matter what culture or language, and our presence had disrupted the remainder of their morning, I am sure.

Traveling with us was a man named Azad, whose skill and demeanor helped us to connect and communicate with the local population. His skills were born from the unique experiences that Azad had lived through growing up in this region. He is Kurdish by birth and had witnessed the horrors of Saddam Hussein upon his people when he was just a teenager. Because of his tenacious resistance during these atrocities, he was jailed by the Iraqis from age fourteen to seventeen. Literally driving nails through his feet did they torture him to reveal his fellow Kurdish comrades in the resistance. He shared with me many other stories of horror that sickened my stomach and brought forth a great deal of emotion diametrically opposed between him and toward the Hussein regime. So while I was fat with the enjoyment of a free society, his young teenage innocence was being profoundly shaped in a very warped manner.

Azad has no need for your or my sympathy; it accomplishes nothing for him or for his people. Rather, he wishes us to see two important facets of his experience. The first being the indomitable spirit of his people to be free and the great cost that has been paid for such freedom. The second being a reappreciation of our own freedom, its attendant cost, and the indomitable spirit of those who have fought to win it and to preserve it. We share an important facet of freedom with the Kurds: the ability for diverse ideologies, philosophies, and religions to peacefully coexist, allowing all to faithfully practice their respective and respectful beliefs.

Later in the day, I was taken to three Christian churches and was able to have a lengthy sit-down meeting with each of their priests. A different story came from each of the interchanges, yet each meeting added a unique color to the pallet of these Christian Kurdish people. Two of the churches, Eastern Catholic, are native to this region and worship in the language of Jesus, Aramaic, and the third is Armenian Orthodox, which worships in Armenian and Kurdish. By the way, if you are interested in learning more about the suffering and faithfulness of other Christians, read about the plight of Armenia and their people.

We were invited to watch the vesper prayer service at one of the Eastern Catholic churches. They accomplished this service in a fashion that mirrors how we, at Saint Paul, hold our Wednesday evening vesper service. In order for religious education to occur, the youth of the parish gather for classes after having participated in the vesper prayer service with their family members. Regardless of culture, only the coupling doctrinal classes with the practice of corporate worship truly complete religious education. How wonderful to see the support of the parents at the vesper service, confirming the truth they themselves, as youths, had learned, as well as confirming the truth that their most precious treasure, their children, were learning. The faith is most effectively passed on through the family unit as they grow together in the grace and knowledge of our Lord Jesus Christ.

Thank you for your prayerful support of the work, which you are accomplishing through me among the soldiers of your nation and among the people of this region. Thank you also for sharing me with our nation's army to temporarily serve the spiritual needs here. I miss you and am expectantly looking forward to our reunion and our work together in the Austin area.

Love, Your Pastor

My dear parish family,

Rejoice, my brothers and sisters, in the faith! Christ is risen! He is risen, indeed! Hallelujah! Our hope indeed is in our crucified and risen Savior!

The water was fifty-five degrees! The air temperature was only sixty-two degrees! It was at this moment that a most profound thought occurred to me: "Why had I volunteered to do this?"

Our youngest soldier, just a few months after her nineteenth birthday and barely eight months since her high school graduation, had conned, cajoled, and pleaded with anyone and everyone within our group to swim with her in the "polar bear relay" at the nearby swimming pool. Assuming that she was an accomplished aquatics athlete, I gladly, if not a little reluctantly, followed her piping to the pool that cool spring day in the first week of March.

Only moments before I was to start this ragtag relay did she informed me that she could barely swim. And by the way, the information coming freely at this point, one of our other fellow relay members could only swim underwater. Unto what had I committed myself? It was only fifty meters, she kept saying as I looked upon our team to see if they were sold the same bill of goods as I. Their expressions confirmed my assumption.

The obligatory dipping of the big toe told my body everything it needed to know: it was very cold, and I would go into shock as soon as my head goes underwater. Would they dare jump in after me or just wait until the summer warmth, knowing the cool water would preserve me quite well? No time to think, the starter's gun sounded, and the screaming began. In I jumped.

The adrenaline rush had caused me to enter the water rather powerfully. The force was such that I began to wear my shorts not too unlike many of the high schoolers back in the States, except they have boxers to cover their buns. Do I stop to adjust my britches, or do I continue because the water is freezing? Decisions at such a time are difficult at best, but in this case, it was downright excruciatingly painful, both for my body and for my pride.

I was able to win this leg of the relay, having chosen to suffer only the pain of my pride, bearing my "cross" so to speak. As I touched my teammate to enter the present bane of my existence, I noticed that it was our "underwater" swimmer who would be paddling on after me. A note about this swimmer, her body fat content would hover somewhere near 0.01 percent and 0.02 percent. Precisely, the cold water zapped her at about the twenty-five-meter mark, and any advantage we may have had upon this cool field had shriveled away.

Our third leg was the spunky nineteen-year-old who didn't swim very well at all. Clinging to the side of the pool for thirty-five of the fifty meters was her mode of movement. Funny, how any compassion for her pain had failed to reach that part of my brain that would feel sorrow for her plight. It was as if those thoughts were carjacked in my synapses by the sense of payback or was it justice, it is all so clouded by memories of cold pain.

We had lost quite a bit of ground, or water, as it were, with our fourth and final leg coming up, slowly. He was built much like the second leg in that he lacked any insulation against such cool water. By the time he had completed his leg, we had finished third from last. Whew! At least we could hold our heads high, proclaiming the undisputed fact of not finishing dead last.

Youth does not always have the wisdom necessary for self-preservation, but their enthusiasm guarantees a good time to be had by all. It will be remembered as a really cool event for even cooler people. Now that is way cool!

Now, to the really cool stuff! Let me share an exciting event in the life of the church and in the life of my friend Keith. His parents never gave Christianity any thought. No spiritual guidance had been offered to him during his youth. Diligently had he been searching for answers by visiting almost every denomination and church that he could, looking for solidly based sincerity and comfort. And although he thought he had tasted every form of Christianity, his quest for truth still left him frustrated. Thinking that he would never find a group of Christians who confessed a faith that stood firmly upon the truths of Scripture, he busied himself reading, comparing, studying, and scouring various publications and the Bible itself.

One day, a Christian gave him a simple booklet known as a small catechism. Adding another piece to his already voluminous repertoire of religious material seemed so habitual, but little did he know the impact of such a concise rendering of the Christian faith found in that little blue booklet. His words were, "Finally, here is summarized what I believe!" As he spoke of this newfound comfort and peace, which stood on the clear teachings of Scripture, his countenance changed. Even though there were many questions asked for further clarification on these teachings with the benefit to be derived centering on the assurance of sins forgiven, he had finally found a home. His home is in the historic, Christian teachings and practice of our beloved synod. Today I had the honor and privilege of baptizing and confirming this man; to God be the glory!

This is the second adult baptism God has brought my way while here in Iraq. What a privilege! Yet work is done not only through the chaplains, but more importantly, it is being done by many of the soldiers themselves. Our Lord Jesus spoke of such an arrangement in order to assure us that His work never rests solely upon our individual shoulders but rather on the shoulders of the church as a whole. "For here the saying holds true, 'One sows and another reaps.' I sent you to reap that for which you did not labor. Others have labored, and you have entered into their labor" (John 4:37–38). Therefore, following the glorious event of his baptism and communion, what will the ripple effect be? How will God's work in this man's life change his family's lives, his coworkers' lives, and the parish family in where he will continue in the faith? Only our heavenly Father knows the answers to such questions. We are just to be faithful messengers in our words to one another and also in our deeds toward one another.

And so we rejoice, He is risen! He is risen, indeed! Hallelujah! Enjoy your family as you remind one another of the resurrection hope we have as Christians; because He lives, we, too, shall live. Tell those you love!

Because we have been joined to Christ in our baptism, though we die, yet shall we live.

I miss being able to celebrate with you this triumphant feast of our Lord. I miss the beautiful music, the organ, brass, winds, strings, and choir! Soon, we shall rejoice in one another's presence.

Love, Your Pastor

My dear parish family,

Sadly, again a young soldier has been killed. Every departed soldier has a story that tears at one's heartstrings. The truck in which this soldier was riding was still drivable after the explosion, and the driver wasn't even injured. The mantra that is cried out to the Lord at every death was present during this memorial ceremony as well: "Why, O Lord?" Help us, we pray, in the middle of things we cannot understand, to believe and find comfort in the communion of saints, the forgiveness of sins, the resurrection of the body, and the life everlasting. Lord, in Your mercy, hear our prayer. The ceremony went on as rehearsed, and comfort was given and comfort was received by all who believe. Thankfully, this young man is rejoicing in heaven as a believer in Jesus Christ, and his family has been and will continue to be comforted by this sure and certain hope in the resurrection.

Events like these crush us and bring an abrupt awakening to the mesmerizing state of the daily routine here in theater. Back home, the five-day work week and the two-day weekend have a way of bringing a cycle to one's life and a means by which one knows what day of the week it is. However, here, one day flows into the next, with the days being consistently twelve to fourteen hours long. There really isn't a weekend or a "day off" from which one can get their bearings straight; one just keeps going, which makes the time seemingly go more quickly. Given such an experience, it is very easy to forget what day of the week it is as well as what date of the month it is. Surreal would be the best word, at times, to describe such an existence.

Later this month, on the twenty-fourth, will be the ninetieth anniversary of the genocide of the Armenian Christians by the Turkish government. It is often forgotten or overshadowed by other horrific crimes of man upon his neighbor; however, this should be noted by us for two reasons.

One, the fact that this heinous act was perpetrated upon our Christian brothers and sisters, and two, that by making note of it, we do all that we can to prevent something of this sort from occurring again. Having mentioned to you about meeting with the Armenian priest and his family who live where they do because of the Diaspora from throughout this region ninety years ago, I bring this to your attention.

Here is a brief history of their plight. The Armenians are an ancient people, having inhabited the highland region between the Black, Caspian, and Mediterranean Seas for nearly three thousand years. They are noted in Greek and Persian sources as early as the sixth century BC. On a strategic crossroads between east and west, Armenia was at various times independent under a national dynasty, autonomous under native princes who paid tribute to foreign powers, or subject to direct foreign rule. The Armenians were the first people to adopt Christianity as a national religion, developing a distinct Indo-European language, alphabet, and national religious culture. The Turkish invasion of Armenia began in the eleventh century AD, and the last Armenian kingdom fell three centuries later. Most of the territories that had once formed the ancient and medieval Armenian kingdoms were incorporated into the Ottoman Empire in the sixteenth century. As a Christian minority, Armenians endured second-class citizenship, including restrictions on many aspects of their participation in society, special taxes, and a prohibition on bearing arms.

During WWI, the Young Turk political faction, from where we get the term "Young Turk," made a secret agreement with Berlin. In return for joining the war against Great Britain, France, and Russia, they sought the creation of a new, ethnically pure Turkish state extending into Central Asia. The ideology called "Pan-Turkism" (creating an homogenous Turkish state) now saw Armenians as an obstacle to the realization of that goal.

On April 24 1915, several hundred Armenian community leaders and intellectuals in Constantinople (Istanbul) were arrested, sent east, and put to death. In May, after mass deportations had already begun, minister of the interior Talaat Pasha, claiming that Armenians could offer aid and comfort to the enemy and were in a state of imminent rebellion, ordered their deportation (after the fact) to "relocation centers"—actually the barren Syrian desert.

Armenians in the Ottoman armies, serving separately in unarmed labor battalions, were removed and murdered. Of the remaining population, the adult and teenage males were separated from the deportation caravans and killed under the direction of Young Turk functionaries. Women and children were driven for months over mountains and desert, often raped, tortured, and mutilated. Deprived of food and water, they fell by the hundreds of thousands along the routes to the desert. Ultimately, more than half the Armenian population, 1,500,000 people, were annihilated. In this manner, the Armenian people were eliminated from their homeland of several millennia. Thousands of refugees scattered throughout the Arab provinces, and the Caucasus died of starvation, epidemic, and exposure. Churches and cultural monuments were destroyed, and small surviving children were renamed and raised as non-Armenians. Interestingly, during Hitler's campaign of genocide with the Jews in WWII, the Turkish leader at that time urged Hitler to not venture down the path of such a genocide. Hitler's response was, "Who remembers now what happened to the Armenians?"

And yet, in all things, we still rejoice that: He is risen! He is risen, indeed! Hallelujah!

Love, your pastor

Hello, Beautiful Birthday Girl,

Oh, how I wish I could be there to celebrate with you. I'm glad you're enjoying your roses. It was fun to surprise you!

Thank you for the Easter package. I'm gobbling up the chocolate, wearing the cool socks and cologne, and have planted the wildflowers package. Hopefully, if they don't get trampled, we'll have a little color blooming in this desert land in a couple of weeks!

Thank you also for all you're doing on the home front. You are such a gracious and giving person, my Carla. Please don't forget to take time for yourself so you are "recharged" and have a little fun in this difficult time. You do amaze and inspire me, my love. Our children are blessed to have you for their mother. What a gift you gave me in our Mariel and our Patrick! I thank Carl and Mary for giving me such a gift in you!

I will call you on Friday evening (my Saturday morning). You are my harbor of peace.

I love and cherish you, Your Mark

My dear parish family,

It all started at a park. It was not the kind of setting, though, that we would normally imagine when we hear of a park, such as manicured lawns, playground equipment, and nicely trimmed hedges. This backdrop at the foot of a nearby mountain range was the site of a thriving Kurdish village at one time. However, due to the cruelty of Saddam Hussein, it had been leveled and its inhabitants either killed or relocated. The only vestiges of their hovels were a few ruins, yet the indomitable spirit of the Kurds was seen in the beautiful large grove of Asian live oaks that silently stood as sentinels guarding over the remains.

At one end of the park, we saw the joyful event of a wedding party with close to two hundred people present. At the other end, we heard the laughter of children who had gathered for another celebration of sorts. Our entourage was situated in the middle of this cacophony of festivities whose sounds fell upon our ears like fresh spring rain upon the parched winter soil. We were being hosted to a picnic by the customs official to honor our LTC, who is in charge of the border logistical operations.

Once our presence was noticed by the nearby children, we were deluged with gawkers. This added attention only grew in intensity when we began to take pictures. Now, every child wanted their picture taken with us, or by us, followed by the obligatory showing of them in the viewfinder. It didn't take long for a soccer game to begin with the Kurdish boys who wished to test the mettle of these American soldiers. We played on a very rocky and unlevel field with a dilapidated soccer ball. What a sight to see! The young Kurdish men were playing in dress pants, dress shirts, and dress shoes. It was a mother's nightmare, especially the boy with the white shirt and the matching pants. Humbly, we barely won this contest, but more importantly we earned their respect and their camaraderie, which, indeed, was priceless.

The spread of food that was placed before us was a Kurdish feast, rice, chicken, lamb, and fresh vegetables. One of the requirements in eating with the Kurds is never to let them see you have a clean plate. For if you do, they refill it with twice as much food as you had before. Serving the meal family style and allowing all to serve themselves from whatever platter is near them was all very acceptable. Dessert was fresh tangerines, bananas, kiwis, and apples—very healthy. Following the meal, the vast majority of the men enjoyed a smoke, and they were very pleased and honored to have received some of the cigars that you have sent to me. How proud they looked to be sharing a cigar with us, as American soldiers.

Coincidentally, one of our hosts was related to the groom at the nearby wedding gala, so we sauntered down to the gathering and were met with broad smiles and backslapping all around. It is also an essential custom for all the guests to drink a strong, sweet hot tea with them. After sipping on two cups of this chai, we were politely pulled into the men's dance line, which was circling around a large drummer and two loud lute players. Joining our pinkie fingers above our heads, we swayed our arms to the beat and uniformly moved our legs in the expectant rhythm. This acquiescence to their hospitality only seemed to embolden them to a more festive mood and gave them a more joy-filled countenance.

The women watched in their beautiful finery of hand-stitched sequined dresses. The older women were staunch in their demeanor, but the younger women enjoyed seeing us Americans clumsily dancing with their husbands and fathers. The bride and groom were at the center of the festivities but were only observers, somewhat like a king and queen. The groom was all smiles, yet the bride in all of her glory was very sullen in appearance. When I inquired as to the bride's seemingly joyless countenance, it was explained to me that during Saddam's terror-filled reign, if the bride appeared happy, she would be dishonored by his soldiers and then given back to the groom. Truly, we do not realize the blessings of living in our democratic freedom here in the States.

In addition to the spiritual care of my soldiers while we were here, your care and love for the Kurdish people, in the form of your packages, were able to be shared with them. With this trip, the remaining parcels of your kindness have now been given out. My plans are to return to this area again in June, July, and August in order to continue any further distribution of your aid to these people. On behalf of the grateful recipients to your goodness, I thank you for your generosity.

One noteworthy expression of gratitude was given to me by an elderly woman who took my hand and kissed it. Pulling my head close to hers, she also kissed my cheek. Her appreciation left me in tears of joy mixed with sorrow for her sufferings. I felt honored by her show of warmth and affection.

God's peace to you on this Good Shepherd Sunday,
Love, Pastor

My dear parish family,

With nearly 3,600 soldiers pulling missions across northern Iraq and having driven over two million highway miles in only four and a half months, we have been blessed with a great deal of safety among our soldiers. The IED devices we watch for on the roads are extremely dangerous, as the insurgents use two to three 155 mm cannon rounds, thereby ensuring that the blast is very effective at accomplishing its evil intent. On another positive note, we also have an excellent combat stress team that provides priceless help to the survivors as they decompress over incidents that inflict harm, not to mention the chaplains and their assistants.

One of the encouraging political events that will be taking place here next week is a major meeting of area mayors, religious leaders, business owners, regional government officials, and other significant people. The outcome of such a gathering is to build consensus, cooperation, and organization for the work we both are accomplishing in this region. As a stabilizing force here in Iraq, we have accomplished and are still accomplishing many beneficial things to further empower the majority, freedom-loving people, to take back their country from the enemies who have tyrannized them for far too long. It is an honor to be a small part of this process, the birth of a free Iraq.

On a humorous note, as a chaplain, one knows when one has finally broken through the trust "barrier" of the soldiers with whom he works when they pull a prank on him. Well, my initiation into their trust came in the form of a certain eight-legged creature common to the desert. Minding my own business in the latrine, I hear outside the door some "lollygagging" going on. Figuring that I needed to finish my business and exit the stall before any "shenanigans" could be pulled, I noticed right beside my foot was a rather large, black scorpion. In one deft movement, I raised my britches and promptly dispatched the intruder that was tossed under the door. Upon my retreat from the stall, my ears were "treated" to the laughter of the boys. My only retort was that they sounded like a bunch of school-girls on the playground. This only seemed to incite their jocularity even further. As you can imagine, the story has been told and retold to all the soldiers about how they "got" the chaplain. I now wear the Scorpion Badge of Courage proudly!

Love, Your Pastor

My dear parish family,

Sadly, the reason I was unable to communicate to you recently was because of a communication blackout due to another attack in our area. One of our Stryker vehicles was hit by a large IED. Outside communication is shut down in order to ensure an authorized contact with the next of kin without anyone else making unauthorized contact with the family. There have been several attacks upon our convoys in a certain area because we are growing in our presence there and we are ruffling the insurgents' tail feathers. We should be well established in strength in about two more months thus allowing one more opportunity for our presence here in Iraq to safeguard the formation of their new government and the founding of freedom from the offenders that have too long run amok here unchecked.

On the home front—my beloved has just let me know that we have finally sold our home in Kansas City! Hooray! The new owners won't take occupancy until the end of June, so Carla has time to get things together, have a yard sale, and anything else in preparation for the short-term lease of an apartment. Then, in August Mariel will be off to Concordia University, Seward, Nebraska, for college, and our household will diminish by one, only to be increased by one when I return sometime in October. We are all very excited and yet apprehensive for another major change in our family's life. That which brings us the most pleasure is that we will return to Austin as a complete unit and not be trying to run two households, per se. God takes such good care of us, even if we are unable to see it; His faithfulness sustains!

My commander has authorized me to come home to Kansas City for R and R in order to be present at Mariel's high school graduation on the twenty-second of May. What an unexpected gift! We are all so elated at the opportunity to be together for a brief time and bask in one another's presence. It will be at least another week before I find out the exact date I will be able to leave the theater. At this point, with this news, I can wait just a bit longer.

The longer one spends interacting with another, the more their trust increases and deepens. When someone opens their soul to you, it leaves you very humbled. When God uses you to share His hope, forgiveness, and love, it leaves you thankful for His grace in that moment. Take the time to interact with other people, starting with your spouse and your children! God has given you not only your family but others with whom to interface so that He can work through your 'clay pot-ness' and accomplish many and wondrous things without you even realizing. Sure, we can see the wreckage we have caused by our sinfulness, but God still uses forgiven sinners to spread His message and to touch other people's lives. Remember, He didn't come to save the righteous, but sinners, like us.

Love, Your Pastor

My dear parish family,

What a precious and memorable time I had with my family, as I was able to attend Mariel's graduation from Lutheran High School and spent a little over a week at home in Kansas City. We decided to celebrate all the holidays we had missed with one another by doing some fine dining at the American Restaurant at Crown Center. It was an evening of lively conversation, laughter, reminiscing, and wonderful food. None of us wanted it to end, and it was difficult to say "goodbye" again, but the time will be short now until I return for good!

With the temperatures rising back here in Iraq, the sand and dust storms that plague this region of the world occur more frequently. The word *storm* needs to be defined, since we are more familiar with it describing a change of temperatures with accompanying wind, rain, thunder, and lightning hullabaloo. However, the only similarity to our depiction of a sandstorm is the severe wind element. Like with the heat, one learns how to live and work in such conditions. It is quite ominous to see a clear day become as dark as night with the arrival of a vast wall of dust and sand enveloping the area. For you northerners, the term "whiteout" describes the lack of visibility associated with a blizzard; here, we use the term "brownout." The real danger occurs for us on the roads as we convoy and move about outside our base. For our aviators, it wreaks havoc on their instruments and equipment and can take them by surprise due to the speed at which such tempests stealthily arise. The good news is that if *we* are having difficulty with movement and visibility, then so are the insurgents.

Speaking of which, we have continued to make progress in greatly reducing the number and severity of attacks in our "hot" region. To compare the last several months with the statistics compiled over the last three years since our arrival, it is an incredible accomplishment. The real victory, I feel, is helping to provide comfort, relief, and safety for the people of this region. The vast majority of the insurgents are not local but are the unwelcome troublers and inciters from surrounding areas. As it is in most unsettled and warring countries, the locals merely wish to maintain their quality of life, enjoying the fruits of their labors and their families. With God's help, I pray the people of this rugged land may return to a time of peace and prosperity.

Love, Pastor

My dear parish family,

When they fired the machine guns from both sides of the aircraft, I was radically shocked out of my daydream. Evidently, out in the middle of the desert, in the hill country, there were some bad guys that should not have been pointing their weapons at us. I didn't hear any incoming fire, only outgoing, so the brief adrenaline rush ended as quickly as it arose, and we smartly moved on toward our destination. Then, just a few days later, one of our helicopters was downed by enemy fire just west of Mosul. The news left me somewhat unsettled about flying again. Thankfully, I have no more flights scheduled, and my sweet wife tells me to stay put! I am the Lord's, and He will do with me what He will whether I am in a helicopter in Iraq, sitting at home with my wife and children, or spending time with you at Saint Paul. God's will be done.

Earlier this week, I was notified by the COSCOM (Corps Support Command) chaplain to remember in prayers one of our sister CSGs (Corps Support Groups) who have had to redeploy all three of their battalion chaplains, one of the chaplains due to health reasons and the other two due to emotional distress. The group chaplain now must cover nearly 3,500 soldiers scattered about for the remainder of his deployment. Hearing about the loss of my fellow chaplains due to the rigors of this deployment reminded me of how fragile we are, regardless of what we think of ourselves and our abilities. Don't we live each day purely by grace? "God chose what is foolish in the world to shame the wise; God chose what is weak in the world to shame the strong…He is the source of your life in Christ Jesus… Therefore, as it is written, 'Let the one who boasts, boast in the Lord'" (1 Cor. 1:27, 30a, 31).

My beloved bride and children have a new abode. They now live in a townhouse, albeit for only about four months. I can only imagine the moving day's activities with the lifting and maneuvering of our household goods. Carla and the kids had trimmed our furnishings somewhat with a recent garage sale, so the total number of rooms to move was somewhat reduced. This should also translate into an easier move to Austin for us upon my return. The kids are enjoying the summer vacation now in full swing for them. Mariel is babysitting and helping with Lutheran High School's summer volleyball league while Patrick is playing on a summer league soccer team and working at the local grocery store. With the sale of our home, the packing of belongings, and the move to the townhouse, Carla's summer can finally slow down a bit. I can't wait to finally be home to help her as well as just be with her and the kids.

Go Longhorns!!! What a great surprise with the men's baseball team winning the college world series in Omaha. I thought it quite interesting that having lost to their state rival, Baylor, three times during the regular season, they were able to beat them twice in two high-pressure games. I bet the tower looked beautiful when it was all lit up with burnt orange lights.

What great and wondrous blessings do we derive from the freedom that is the hallmark of our great nation. As you enjoy your family and your friends over the weekend of the Fourth, continue to be mindful of the great sacrifices that all those faithful veterans before us have given in order to insure and continue the joys we are celebrating. Yet these freedoms are not the greatest gift we have received. For the penultimate freedom we have received is bought for us through our Savior. Through the blood of Jesus, we have been freed from fear, guilt, and everlasting punishment. As you enjoy hearing again the great news of this freedom at Saint Paul, rejoice that we are also free to gather and proclaim this hope to a dead and dying world. "Live as people who are free, not using your freedom as a cover-up for evil, but living as servants of God. Honor everyone. Love the brotherhood. Fear God. Honor the emperor" (1 Pet. 2:16–17)

Love, Pastor

My dear parish family,

We have been thoroughly indoctrinated in the ways of the *shamals* here in northern Iraq. Shamals are the dust/sandstorms that plague this region of the world from June through the end of September. They usually build a billow of sand and dust between three thousand and eight thousand feet high and can last up to ten days, with the average being about three days in length. We just experienced our first shamal that lasted more than twenty-four hours. With the dust and sand acting like a seal over the region, the temperatures did not cool down in the evenings but instead remained in the upper nineties all night. One would think that we would remember our moniker "always an adventure"; however, just when we think we have experienced it all, something new comes along!

Having had a great deal of interaction with my colonel in recent days, allow me to share with you a thought that he had been shown by the Lord regarding this deployment. He said, "You go to war with the staff and soldiers you've been given." He made this declaration when the Lord had brought him to realize that his expectations of himself and his staff and his soldiers were markedly different from what God had wanted to accomplish in him and through him. The application of this paradigm for us in our parish, and for that matter, in any parish, is that we are to work with and through one another with all of our accompanying idiosyncrasies in order to realize those things that our Lord has given us to carry out.

As a parish family, we are united around and bound together with the teachings of our Lord and not our peculiarities. We confess that blessed union as we gather around the altar of our Lord. Having been given such a communion with one another around the same sweet forgiveness, let us boldly work together in kindness and in gentleness, as in a marriage. And thus, like marriage, being in such close proximity with each other, as we labor together, can reveal the ugliness of our own sins. Having it revealed then, let it lead us to repent and to commune together again around the altar with the same broken sinners with whom we have been gathering, receiving again His sweet forgiveness. Thus, we are enabled to continue together in the Lord's work in spite of our foibles. Consider this undeniable truth; we did not choose those with whom we are united in the one true faith, we were given them by our gracious Father along with our faith. Let us, therefore, cherish our union in our common confession of this one true faith.

Through the grapevine I hear that you all will be sending the soldiers and the locals some wonderful boxes of things to share with one another. I thank you in advance for your commitment to serving these men and women of our military as well as the Iraqis and the Kurds. Next week I will be taking the last of my supplies to the Kurds of the border towns in northern Iraq. What a joy it is to be used by you to share your goodness.

Our Sunday morning services here have been such a joy in which to be a part. Just like at home, there is a core group who make it almost every Sunday, and then there are the ten to twenty others who come and go due to their daily schedules or the convoy operations of their unit. There is a great deal of shared strength and support from gathering together to hear the Word made flesh, isn't there? Even though we do not have a pianist every Sunday, we still belt out the hymns without any accompaniment and receive comfort from the priceless words with which they have been penned. Recently, we sang "The Lord's My Shepherd, Leading Me" (*LW* 417). The last verse brought great solace: "I take my stand forevermore within my Shepherd's fold, secure in His forgiving love. How gently strong His hold! He loves me so He leads me to His blessings rich and bold." What comfort these old hymns bring that remain on the lips of His children.

God's peace to you all, Pastor

My dear parish family,

Harsh living conditions seem to age people in an accelerated manner. Existing in tents for the past year, the small village of families was making it work even though they owned relatively nothing of notable mention. Their daily supply of water was prominently positioned in the center of the camp in six large stainless steel containers. Here, the women gathered for this vital substance, waiting patiently for their three- to five-gallon pitchers (approximately twenty-five to forty pounds each) to be filled; two of the women were expecting within the month. This scene has been played out for millennia, and yet, in our modern times, seeing such a sight leaves me in awe of the conveniences I take for granted every day. Their reception of our presence was humbling. And their appreciation for the donations you gathered and sent was unmistakable. One of the biggest hits for this trip was handing them a Polaroid snapshot of each of them with their children. To show their appreciation, a young man came around to us with an aluminum pitcher of cold juice for us to drink. We had to lay aside our fears of drinking something that may have been mixed with unbottled water in order to receive such an offer of thanks with equal gratitude and deal with the intestinal consequences later. It is hard to describe the beautiful countenance of those who received your outpouring of love. Once again, you have shown Christ's love to these formerly oppressed people; be convinced, our small efforts are not in vain.

At the next village, we were greeted with the sight of one of the young sons running about enjoying a brief respite from diaper and all clothing. We smiled as the slightly embarrassed mother scooped him up and took him to their small hovel. Slowly, this village has rebuilt since Saddam's regime leveled it in the nineties. Their congenial response was a platter filled with cups of cold yogurt or buttermilk. It is a common drink here. Again, our intestinal fortitude was challenged as we drank the milky concoction.

The young men and women who have accompanied me on these humanitarian missions, becoming your hands and faces of love and outreach, have themselves been touched and influenced by their participation. Some have little or no church background. Following our expeditions, there is a great deal of sharing their stories with one another and a joy in serving others. These opportunities open the door to sharing the faith. Rejoice in His grace as He uses such instruments as you and me!

Love, Pastor

My dear parish family,

Flag football in Iraq? Maybe, but how about flag football in Iraq with local Iraqi Kurds? Now, that would be something! After an intense hour of instruction with a local soccer club in the town of Zahko, we attempted a friendly game of flag football between two mixed teams made up of American soldiers and the local soccer club. What a hoot! To my surprise, they picked up the basics quite rapidly, but having observed rugby from the Brits, whenever they were about to have their flag pulled, they would laterally throw the football to one of their teammates. We had some uproariously big belly laughs over the antics, by both the Americans and the Iraqi Kurds, which were exhibited on that green soccer field. Following the game, we were quickly drawn into a pick-up soccer game with the same mixed teams. It was sheer beauty to witness the finesse and the grace with which these sixteen- to twenty-year-old boys played. Truly, a good time was had by all as the sun began to set that evening.

On the next day, when we were delivering the nearly two HMMWVs full of goods, we were treated to an afternoon picnic by the clear Habur River. Again, we were escorted around by the president of the region and some of his staff. For the first time since that crazy "polar bear relay" back in March, I was able to go swimming, albeit in my boxers, but nevertheless it was an enjoyable afternoon. We taught the men how to throw a Frisbee and played a game of "keep away." We were quite a sight, very untanned bodies in boxers throwing a Frisbee in an Iraqi river. No, there weren't any incriminating pictures to share.

On a more sobering note, I was privileged to have met a Kurdish LTC who had served his army for more than thirty-three years. He told me he was from a family of ten boys who all fought together against Saddam's regime during the last thirty years of severe oppression. With moistened eyes, he also shared with me that he is the only surviving brother of the ten; Saddam's regime murdered the other nine. He humbled me by his sharing of these painful memories and by his great pride in hosting us as American soldiers. When he learned that we had been out visiting some of the surrounding villages with supplies, he clapped his hands together and beamed with appreciation and gratitude, for many of the same villages are just now getting back on their feet after the death and destruction that reigned here earlier. We are accomplishing a great deal of benefit with our presence and with your participation in this outreach.

With many Christian villages dotting the countryside, the term for their religious leaders is not a pastor but rather a priest. Therefore, explaining to the locals in northern Iraq about what I am and what my job is as a chaplain is more understandable and translatable to them with the moniker "priest." Rarely have the local Muslims ever talked with a priest, so there has been some wonderful interchanges between myself and them via an interpreter. They are not anti-Christian but rather very respectful and just ignorant of Christians. There are some villages and, obviously, many towns where Muslims and Christians peacefully and prosperously coexist. Mostly, it is in these very small villages where one religion is central to the village, yet acceptance of others abounds.

Love, Your Pastor

My dear parish family,

Your families are the most important earthly gift that your beloved Father has given you. Your family is a microcosm of your church. In fact, the family is the smallest unit of the church. Here, in the family, is where you and I were trained in Christian teaching and living by our parents. Nevertheless, either with pride or humility, our families/marriages are the single most important earthly gift given to us to cherish and to honor and to love. Unfortunately, I have met with soldiers who tell me their biological families are so dysfunctional and toxic they have had to become estranged. I grieve for them. Thankfully, many are blessed to have married into a healthy family or have found other meaningful relationships. These people, though they share no DNA, become the family I refer to.

For what do you wish to be remembered upon your death? That you received certain academic degrees, or that you were the head of a company or department, or that you traveled hither and yon, or would you rather only be remembered as a faithful husband or wife, son or daughter, and father or mother? Truly, such an achievement is much less glamorous, but it is also a much more challenging and a far more rewarding aspiration with consequences that can profoundly affect future generations.

This last month has brought me much weariness and heaviness of heart. Six of my soldiers ranging in age from early twenties to midthirties are having serious marriage and family problems. The quick judgment is that it must be due to the deployment and separation. However, other older and wiser chaplains have confirmed my suspicions, if the marriages were somewhat "on the rocks" before the deployment, then the deployment has grave potential to drive such a marriage and a family to the brink. Seeing the pain, the anger, the resentment, the betrayal, and the grief deeply plowed into these young soldiers' countenances over their family crises and knowing that I am helpless to assist from afar gives me such sorrow.

Cherish your families. Invest your God-given gift of time and energy into your marriages and into your families. Over what will we lament, and with what will we desire to be surrounded upon as we await death? Will it be that we should have spent more time or energy upon our career and, thus, surround ourselves with our accomplishments? Will it be that we should have earned more money and, thus, surround ourselves with our beautiful possessions? Or will it be that we ought not to have struggled for anything earthly and, thus, only be surrounded by our greatest gift, our spouse and our family and the gift God bestows, Word and Sacrament in the church?

Please don't let my seriousness overwhelm you. But do take note of this most important reminder for you and for me. We need to repent to our spouses and our families, receiving from them the blessed absolution of their forgiveness for our sins as their spouses and as their parents. "The saying is trustworthy and deserving of full acceptance, that Christ Jesus came into the world to save sinners, of whom I am the foremost. But I received mercy for this reason, that in me, as the foremost, Jesus Christ might display His perfect patience as an example to those who were to believe in Him for eternal life" (1 Tim. 1:15–16). As a parish family made up of many families, this IS what we are all about, for it IS what our Lord is all about.

Love, Pastor

My dear parish family,

Your kind generosity of "goodies" for my soldiers and the wonderful supplies sent for the local Iraqis and Kurdish people continue to amaze me and my unit; you have made a memorable impression upon them! The other individuals whom your goodness has continued to astonish have been all of my contacts up north through whom I distribute your aid; to have such strong Christian witness of generosity and outreach has been quite a statement to these people of our desire to be a part of their "rebirth" toward a free nation. Thank you for allowing me to be a part of your generosity to so many. It has been such a joy.

In Iraq this month, the constitution for the new Iraqi government is being finished and will be voted upon by all the provinces in October. From everything we are hearing, this procedure is going quite well, especially since many of the Sunnis have jumped aboard and have finally become involved in this normal act of a democratic society. Now, if in October the provinces approve this newly written constitution, then there will be general elections in December for all of the various officials in this new Iraqi democratic government. Exciting, indeed, is all that has been accomplished by the brave Iraqi people who have risked much in order to bring this concept of freedom unto a reality for their nation. The biggest problem that continues to plague this new government's movement forward has been the religious extremists, such as from Syria, Iran, Jordan, etc. Interestingly enough and not always reported to you via the news is that very few of these problem terrorists come from within the Iraqi nation.

Another positive sign of the wonderful progress in the turnaround of the public's confidence has been the large increase in vehicular traffic on the main roads. When we first arrived, the traffic upon the major highways was very sporadic. However, in the last several months, the busyness of the locals traveling upon their highways has dramatically increased, a confident sign of a confident people regarding their beloved nation. The only downside to this wonderful news is that it causes more headaches for our convoys moving through the traffic safely. With progress always comes such "good headaches," doesn't it?

Having been taking advantage of reading some of Martin Luther's works, I came across a wonderful thought which he expressed regarding Christ dwelling only with sinners. He spoke of every page of the New Testament containing testimony that Christ's proper office is to save sinners, to seek and save the lost. And the entire work of Jesus—from the days when He was in Galilee and, to the amazement and alarm of the Pharisees, ate with tax collectors and sinners; to the moment when He, in contradiction with the principles of every rational morality, promised paradise to the thief on the cross—yes, His entire life on earth, from the cradle to the cross, is one unique, grand demonstration of a wonder beyond all reason: the miracle of divine forgiveness, of the justification of the sinner. Christ dwells only among sinners. As Luther put it:

> Be careful never to endeavor to obtain such purity that you no longer find yourself a sinner, much less desire to be one. *Christ dwells only among sinners.* This is why He descended from heaven, where He dwelt among the righteous, so also to make His dwelling among sinners. Take note of His love time and time again, and you will experience the sweetest consolation…And so only in Him, through having despaired of yourself and your works, will you find peace. Here you will learn from Christ himself, that He, as He has received you unto Himself, has made your sins His own, and His righteousness your righteousness.

It is the service of us as the Church today to cry out this wonderfully Good News. Can we do this? Is the gospel of justification of the sinner through faith alone still the bread from which we live? Is it still the heart and soul of our preaching? Do we still know—or once again realize!—what sin is, how serious the judgment of God is, and what a fearful thing it is to fall into the hands of the living God? Do we still know the full consolation of faith in the Savior of sinners, in the way Luther's explanation of the Second Article of the Apostles' Creed shows Him to us? Do we know what it means that this Christ is actually present in the Word of His Gospel and in His Sacrament, as near to us as He was when He walked the earth, yes, nearer than when He ate with tax collectors and sinners? If we still know all of this, if we still believe it, is it a living possession, or has it become a mere tradition? Have they become words without content? These are the questions that the Reformer puts to us as Evangelical Lutherans. As Luther put it so well, "We are beggars; that is true!" So must we answer with shame and remorse. But immeasurably rich in mercy is He who is the Savior of all sinners and whom the New Testament once called "the Savior of His body" (Eph. 5:23), the Redeemer of His church. And inexhaustible are the riches of His means of grace, the Gospel in sermon and absolution, Holy Baptism, and the Holy Supper—inexhaustible for all beggars!

Love, your Pastor

My dear parish family,

Again, I write on a difficult subject matter. He was only nineteen years old, but he handled himself as if he was much older. He was a gunner on one of our Stryker attack vehicles (note the attached pictures). He was very faithful in attending Sunday chapel services, but because of his quiet nature, he was easy to overlook in the crowd. Studying his Bible regularly, he often asked questions regarding a certain passage or related an interesting insight from his reading. Asking if he could take a Bible to give it to a fellow soldier was an example of his quiet way of evangelizing. Last Thursday night, he excitedly reported that his friend had read the entire Old Testament in a little over a day, except for the Psalms and Proverbs! His friend had commented that there wasn't enough action in the Psalms and the Proverbs to keep his attention. How exciting to see such enthusiasm coming from this quiet kid for sharing his faith and the Scriptures with his fellow brothers in arms.

With seemingly unusual poetic *injustice*, the day after he turned nineteen, he went outside the wire into the city of Mosul on a mission with his Stryker team. While guarding over an Iraqi police station, standing in the open hatch of his Stryker vehicle with only his head and shoulders showing, he was killed by an expert enemy sniper from about three hundred meters away. He died instantly and painlessly in the arms of his fellow soldiers. As my heart broke again, I asked, did this young man die in vain? Was his presence here in Iraq purposeless? Then, resoundingly, after a moment of anger at the loss of one more precious life, I acknowledged as a fellow believer who will see this brother of mine in heaven, I loudly and confidently confessed, "NO!" I was blessed to have seen God's hidden work in this man's life as well as through this man's quiet witness. Though

I do not always have such a clear and obvious example, I know by faith that all who labor in the Lord's vineyard labor not in vain.

Therefore, you and I who also labor in this same Lord's vineyard DO NOT labor in vain. Simply because we do not see purpose or measurable results in the work unto which we have put our shoulders DOES NOT negate the worth and God's purpose for our sharing this one true faith with our family and with our friends. God has chosen to work through His holy Word, which we feebly proclaim. He has especially chosen His preached Word and the Sacraments to be THE place to find Him, THE place to come in contact with Him, THE place to be joined to Him, and THE place to have a personal relationship with Him.

Continue to ask your friends to join you at church. Help them with the liturgy, just as your parents or friends helped you. Tell them why your parish is so precious to you. Explain to them from the Scriptures and your catechism the eternal and universal truths that we faithfully proclaim and you joyfully believe. Remind them that this truth is not a new or different truth, for there is only ONE truth, and we, as God's people, are only carrying that mantle of this one truth from those whom we have received it. Get involved in these people's lives, and allow them to be involved in yours so that we can build one another up in this one truth faith and so that we can faithfully pass it on to our children and grandchildren.

There have been other soldiers, in addition to this young man, who have valiantly and willingly given their lives for their friends, for their country, and for the people of the Iraqi nation. These unsung heroes have been used by God to fulfill the request that we regularly pray in the Lord's Prayer: "Thy Kingdom come, Thy will be done on earth as it is in heaven." How profoundly humbling it is for us to grapple with St. Paul's proclamation: "For none of us lives to himself, and none of us dies to himself. If we live, we live to the Lord, and if we die, we die to the Lord. So then, whether we live or whether we die, we are the Lord's. For to this end Christ died and lived again, that He might be Lord both of the dead and of the living" (Rom. 14:7–9).

Regardless of whether such seeming injustice makes sense to our minds, God has used, is using, and will continue to use them, and to use us in the extension of His kingdom. And on Judgment Day, we all, like the sheep in the parable, will answer, "Lord, when did we see You hungry and feed You, or thirsty and give You drink? And when did we see You a stranger and welcome You, or naked and clothe You? And when did we see You sick or in prison and visit You?" And the King will answer us, "Truly, I say to you, as you did it to one of the least of these my brothers, you did it to Me." May it be done unto us as You have said, we are the Lord's servants.

> In God, my faithful God, I trust when dark my road;
> Great woes may overtake me, yet He will not forsake me.
> It is His love that sends them; at His best time He ends them.
> > If death my portion be, it brings great gain to me;
> > It speeds my life's endeavor to live with Christ forever.
> > He gives me joy in sorrow, come death now or tomorrow.
> > > 'So be it,' then, I say with all my heart each day.
> > > Dear Lord, we all adore You, we sing for joy before You.
> > > > Guide us while here we wander until we praise You
> > > > Yonder. (*LW* 421)

Love, Pastor

My dear parish family,

On the home front, change has come upon my beloved bride's life and indirectly to my life as well. Carla took Mariel to Concordia University in Seward, Nebraska, last Thursday for freshman orientation, with classes to begin on Monday. For many of you who have already gone through this chapter in your life, you are very well acquainted with the emotions that accompany such changes in the household as you see a child spread their wings and fly. Patrick started school as a junior at Lutheran High in Kansas City. The school has moved to a new and beautiful facility. Patrick has been attending soccer practice for the last couple of weeks in preparation for their first game; he may be playing goalie or left wing. He will be driving himself and a friend to school in my black '94 Impala SS. He is a good driver, so I am not too concerned; besides, if he can handle the traffic in and around Austin during rush hour, he can surely handle Kansas City's traffic. While my Carla is experiencing these events firsthand, I will be encountering it fully upon my return. I am more than ready to return and begin this next phase of life with my family and with you, my flock.

This process of democratization for which the citizens in Iraq are striving will, however, take time. It took Europe a millennium and a half to resolve its post-Roman Empire crisis of social and political identity, nearly a thousand years to settle on the nation-state form of political organization, and nearly five hundred years more to determine which nations were entitled to be states. The continuing crisis in the Middle East in our time may prove to be nowhere near so profound or so long lasting. However, in the western world, the political assumption of a secular government is an alien creed in a region most of whose inhabitants, for more than a thousand years, have avowed faith in a Holy Law that governs all of life, including government and politics. If this continues in full force, then the twenty-first century Middle East will eventually be seen to be in a situation similar to Europe's in the fifth century AD, when the collapse of the Roman Empire's authority in the west threw its subjects into a crisis of civilization that obliged them to work out a new political system of their own. God willing, we have the fortitude to see this through in order to protect and preserve the freedom for which so many in this nation have died.

Love, Your Pastor

My dear parish family,

Some of my soldiers were given quite a treat last week by a thankful doctor from the nearby village. Some of the supplies that you have so faithfully and lovingly sent have been distributed through this local doctor to his village and to many other smaller villages for which he is responsible in the vicinity. In gratitude for our generosity and assistance, he organized an outing for these soldiers. This outing was to visit and explore a very ancient and historical site known as Al Hatra.

Hatra was a strategic city that controlled an access route from the west to the east through this region of Iraq. The ruins that we took in date back to nearly 200 BC and were a part of an empire run by the Parthians, about whom Scripture speaks, especially in the book of Acts. Quite impressive, indeed, was the sheer size and the engineering of its nearly twenty feet thick walls and its fifty feet high buildings. Sadly, over the centuries of the various political and governmental upheavals, the site, like so many around the world, had been ravaged by looters and plunderers. However, it still was an amazing adventure to walk among its ruins and its history. When Iraq becomes more stable, her tourism industry should be utilized, since there are some extraordinary archeological sites and remains that could be preserved and displayed.

Hatra also has a more recent and tragic history associated with it. Not long after our stabilization of this region, US-led investigators located nine trenches containing hundreds of bodies believed to be Kurds killed during the repression by Saddam's regime in the 1980s. Skeletons of unborn babies still in their mothers' womb's as well as toddlers clutching toys were unearthed. Usually, mass graves contain only men of fighting age, but Saddam's regime was of a more twisted type. Let there be no doubt that our presence here has helped to bring legitimacy to these silent deaths and has allowed the people of Iraq to regain control of their nation from such oppression.

With our unit and a few others who are getting closer to our departure dates, we have begun scheduling the train up for our replacements. They should be arriving soon to begin the transition from our leadership to theirs. To have such an influx of more soldiers crowds the housing possibilities present on our base. Therefore, in a couple of weeks, we will be moving into more temporary structures in order to accommodate the new units' arrival. No one is grousing about such change since it only serves to further validate our impending redeployment, for we are only a month away from our flight out of here to Kuwait, the first leg of our trip home.

Your cards, letters, emails, and packages to me have been a great source of comfort and strength for which I am very grateful; thank you. I, too, am so excited about my return to Austin and to St. Paul, but especially to do so with my family.

Love, Your Pastor

My dear parish family,

I have begun giving out the book *To All Eternity*, a very fine Concordia Publishing House book that was purchased with funds managed by the Endowment Committee. They have been very warmly received by the soldiers within my unit. In our weekly command and staff meetings, I regularly use fine art depicting an event from the Scriptures along with any of the pertinent information that I am briefing. So when some of the officers who are present at these briefings saw the beautiful artwork inside these books, they commented to me of how they remember some of the paintings from my slides in those weekly briefings. Thank you, again, for allowing me to be the vessel through whom you served, loved, and blessed these soldiers over the last twelve months.

Next week we will be moving out of our "tin can" storage containers into the transient housing bays where we will be spending our remaining days before our movement back to the good ol' USA! Privacy will be given up for a large bay where all the males are housed and all the females in a different bay. On the positive side of this arrangement is the increased opportunity for our unit to reconnect before we part ways to the "four corners" of the States. Such a living condition is also very conducive for conversations about God. This brings up an important life lesson that has been regularly imparted in this environment: finding something of value or worth in a situation that seems to be without any redeemable qualities or at least any worth mentioning. There have been immeasurable joys and crushing wretchedness. I have learned a great deal about myself, the hardships of war, and the toughness that God has created within the human spirit. God's mercy and grace is always surrounding us no matter the circumstances.

Love, your Pastor

My dear parish family,

Our replacements have arrived, and we have begun our training transition process with them. Though they have experience at doing the jobs of my soldiers, one can still see the trepidation with which they arrived. As I reflect upon the emotions and the consternation of taking over this mission nearly a year ago, I am sure we looked and acted the same way. It is hard to believe that our year here is about over. The first ninety days were full of excitement and newness with homesickness remaining at arm's length. However, then came the next ninety days when it all came crashing in upon us. How interesting and, at times, almost unbearable to experience such a broad spectrum of inner sensations. The next ninety days followed with a type of numbness that accompanies the resignation of being here for the duration. Now, with each passing week, the fog of resignation begins to lift, and the sunshine of our final days has begun to break through, illuminating the reality of our departure. Yee-haw!!!

My final trip to the Iraqi-Turkish border to deliver your blessings to these people went smoothly. We were able to revisit the "tent-village" that we had been to during our last adventure up north. How appreciative these people were to receive the clothing and other articles of beneficial nature, especially with their winter approaching in a matter of a few months. We played some soccer with the young boys who had just received one of the soccer balls we had just given out. There is nothing like playing with kids that helps to strengthen a relationship with them as well as with their parents. How true it is: if you love their kiddos, you love them.

It has also been a joy to have seen how the prosperity of this region has continued to flourish since our first trip up here nearly nine months ago. Traffic is thicker, new building is going on, improvements on the infrastructure continue, and products are available to the people that were never available before. Again, it is a reassurance that our presence here as well as the work of the interim government continues to make progress, albeit slowly, but nevertheless progress.

Saying goodbye is always a difficult thing to do with having allowed our hearts, both the Iraqi Kurds and ours, to have become intertwined. Impressed and humbled by their kindness and generosity; we have gotten the sense that the goodwill we have brought will not be forgotten, especially among the next generation. These youngsters have been able to see their nation be "reborn," as it were, and will be the ones whose spirit will keep it moving upward and forward. God willing, they will be able to continue what their parents and grandparents have begun.

My love to you, Your Pastor

My dear parish family,

With a flurry of activity, our week began. Our replacement unit has been working diligently to learn the description and nuance of each position here in the harsh deployed environment. Watching the officers and leaders of the various sections has revealed an interesting behavior that is exhibited during such a transfer of authority: the one who is taking over the operation questions almost everything, either silently or verbally, which the attendant unit has been doing for the last year, regardless of the reasons. In essence, there is a questioning of ability and competency. And then, the reverse is revealed in my officers and leaders of these various sections: the ones leaving look down upon these "newbies" as merely being those who think they know it all but haven't been here for the year that we have; therefore, they do not know anything. It all can be summarized with the sin of pride or vanity. Yet, is is also based on true concern for those taking over our positions and the locals who we have come to love. On the part of the departing unit, in that they perceive themselves as knowing it all since they have put in their time here, having tried many and different options, and on the part of the incoming unit, in that they have an objective view, not being blinded by the subjective-ness of being too close to the issues. I am sure many of you can relate this to various situations either at work or at home. How useful and welcomed during such relinquishment of responsibility would humility and kindness be. Instead of saying to oneself, "God, I thank You that I am not like other men…" we would say, "God, be merciful to me, a sinner!" Then would our Lord say, "I tell you, this man went down to his house justified, rather than the other. For everyone who exalts himself will be humbled, but the one who humbles himself will be exalted" (Lk 18:11ff).

With the increase of traffic due to the arrival of soldiers, the availability of fuel, and the overall safety of the roads due to our stabilizing effort, there has been a vigilant effort made to move safely and quickly through such traffic with our convoys without accidents or incidents. At the same time, there has been an increase by the insurgents with vehicle-borne IEDs attempting to infiltrate our convoys. Responding to such an increase in this type of enemy activity, our convoys are trained to use many and various methods to control traffic, which have been received by the locals with compliance and cooperation. However, if someone tries to cut into our line or speed around us, then one of the stronger methods of determent is to fire a warning shot in the ground immediately in front of the offending vehicle so as to prevent any possible harm done to both the convoy and the local national. Unfortunately, one such incident recently occurred and with it the rare result unfolded before the gunner's eyes: a ricochet off of the ground and a striking of an innocent local national. The Iraqi was cared for and stabilized by our medevac and field hospital. The gunner, a twenty-year-old, was visibly shaken at what he saw transpire before his eyes and by what took place at his very hands. After a very long talk and prayer, we had to send him and his convoy partners back to their base the next morning. All of the accounts I have shared over the year are based on the sometimes ugly realities of war.

Soon, I will finally be reunited with my beloved bride after nearly twenty-one months of "off and on" separation. I am very ready for this blessed reunion but realize that I need to be sure to decompress after all that has transpired here over the last year in order to give to my family the best I have to offer, as well as you, my parish family. This letter will probably be my next to last letter from Iraq, hopefully. You all have been a strength to me and to my family, thank you so very much. God be praised for the blessed communion in which He has placed us.

Love, Your Pastor

PART V
COMING HOME!

My dear parish family,

As our work here has finally wound down and as our replacement unit continues to take over our operation, we've been enabled to have more time to relax in the afternoons and evenings. The early fall weather has been more than cooperative so that these social events are more enjoyable. The highs have been between 100–105 in the shade, and the lows have been in the 80s.

And here, if you will allow me some musings regarding God's beautiful grace for us, His people. God's grace is His freely offered gift of forgiveness. Undeserved, unmerited, incapable of being repaid, and open to being unappreciated and misused is God's grace. If it does not fall under these categories, then it isn't grace, but rather it is merit. Merit is anything that is due us because of something we have done to earn it. Or it is defined as the ability of returning the favor/gift.

In the military, as in much of life, nothing is for free. There are always strings attached to any gift. "What is the expected response for such a gift?" is always our question upon receiving something from someone. Since we feel beholden to them for that kindness, we desire to pay it back. The desire to "pay it back" in thanksgiving is not necessarily wrong, but how will we know that we have done all that is necessary to pay it back? Again, we are left with uncertainty. Grace is incapable of being "paid back." It can only be received. Its enormity is supposed to be overwhelming, because Christ was damned for us, because Christ received the divine wrath from the Father for us, because Christ willingly and obediently accomplished this for us for no other reason than to free us from such just and right condemnation. If grace could be "paid back," then it never really was given to us as grace.

The standard is the norm, but what do we do when we break that standard? There are basically two possibilities with which we respond. Either we allow ourselves "wiggle room" with the standard and lower the standard by justifying what we have done with our vain excuses. Or we realize the futility of our attempts to maintain such an impeccable standard and confess our inherent lack.

Confessing our inherent lack of ability to fulfill the standard does not change the standard but instead allows the standard to stand, unbent by our excuses thereby removing all possible "wiggle room" of excuses, allowing us to see ourselves in need of God's grace. Such a disclosure is very disconcerting, because we are faced with who we are in light of an immovable and, at this point, condemning standard.

Hence, Christ came and lived the perfect life in every thought, in every word, and in every deed in order to cover over our thoughts, words, and deeds. Yet there is more to be paid to the Father than just a perfectly lived life. Christ had to be damned for us, since that is the just punishment for our sins and for our sinfulness. God's wrath was appeased and God's justice fulfilled by Christ's life and by Christ's death. His resurrection from the dead is proof that the Father is pleased with the Son's payment for us.

This accomplishment covers all of mankind, whether they believe it or not. It covers the Adolph Hitlers, the Saddam Husseins, and other such wretched human beings as we. That is grace!

Some great illustrations for grace and mercy exemplified are from the words of our dear Lord Jesus in two of His parables and in His last act of mercy from His cross. The first parable is from Luke 15:11–31, the Parable of the Prodigal Son. The father in the parable receives his son back without any repercussions of the son's actions. He does this all by grace, and we know it to be grace because of the elder son's reaction to the father's free gift of grace. The elder son thought the father's action to be unfair or unjust. That is the definition of the grace of God toward us, and it is toward us because of Christ's life, death, and resurrection.

The second parable is from Luke 18:9–14, the Parable of the Pharisee and the Tax Collector. The tax collector comes before the Lord, ashamed of what he is without Christ's life lived for him, without Christ's death died for him, and without Christ's resurrection accomplished for him. Being ashamed, he can only plead for mercy, and he is also exampled as having a proper posture toward God. The Pharisee, on the other hand, does not view himself as being that bad of a person, because he thanks God that he is not like other "bad" people. The tax collector confesses his utter sinfulness and does not compare himself to anyone so as to avoid taking away from the great gift of grace that covers all of his sins. We are either totally corrupt and in need of total forgiveness, or we are not. If we are not totally corrupt, then we do *not* totally need the Father's forgiveness found in Christ. If we are totally corrupt, regardless of how we compare with others, then we *are* totally in need of the Father's forgiveness found in Christ. And He bestows it upon us lavishly!

Finally, the thief on the cross who asks for mercy and forgiveness in his request to be remembered by Christ when Christ comes into His kingdom is answered by our Lord with an affirmative: "Today, you will be with me in paradise." Read about the dialog between the thieves and with Christ on the cross in Luke 23:39–43.

Love, Pastor

My dear parish family,

When we arrived at Fort Riley on a cool and wet early morning, the smells and the sights were somewhat overwhelming after such austere surroundings in and around our base. In a matter of a few days, we quickly finished our out-processing and were bused to Kansas City for a reunion ceremony complete with the local media of radio, television, and newspaper. Our families were all present for the festivities and celebrations at which we received our military awards and ribbons for a job well done while we were deployed. I was honored to have received the Bronze Star from our commanding general. It was heaven on earth to bask in the presence of my dear family, and the public celebrations and awards took a back seat to their beautiful smiles!

One of the more memorable receptions took place as we flew through the Dallas/Fort Worth Airport. Upon our arrival, we were honored with an archway of water shooting over the entire plane from two airport firetrucks. What a glorious sight! Then upon our entry into the terminal building, volunteers from the VFW and the American Legion greeted us warmly with handshakes and clapping. How humbling to receive such a "red carpet" treatment. I couldn't help but recall some of my fellow soldiers' stories as they told of the lack of warmth and lack of respect they received when returning from Vietnam.

Now, having been home for approximately a week, I find that my head is still spinning, as I am "coming down" from the tempo of life which I have just left. During this transition time, Carla and I have a few short trips planned, including one to see Mariel in Nebraska, Patrick's soccer games to attend, and a few moments to catch up on with one another before we, three, return to Austin. God willing, we should be down in Austin by

November 3 with my first Sunday back in the pulpit on Sunday, November 13.

Thank you all so very much for all that you did for me and for my beloved Carla, Mariel, and Patrick. Your support and prayers have been priceless as I have traversed the entire spectrum of feelings and emotions being apart from family. I am looking forward with great anticipation to once again be your pastor, preaching for you, teaching you and your children, and enjoying the fellowship of the saints as we gather to be fed and nourished from the great Shepherd.

Love, Your Pastor

My Dear Ones,

What an unusual phone call. The USARC headquarters in Atlanta, which has a public affairs office, telephoned me regarding a possible television interview about my tour of duty in Iraq. This interview would take place in New York City with FOX News and with CNN and possibly with other media. Four days before I would even fly out, I learned that this possibility had become a reality. Quickly calling our head elder and making plans with our church secretary and with our organist, I was able to then set in place the necessary things so that the midweek Advent service could go on without a hitch.

Traveling to New York City by jet was a first, as well as commandeering a taxi for the trip from La Guardia to midtown Manhattan. Arriving at the Marriott on Times Square was magical. Sights, sounds, and smells stimulated my senses to overload in this amazing city. I was humbled to have been picked to do such a thing on the government's dime. The gentleman with whom I was seated on the flight to New York City was a Turk from the island of Cypress, a divided island of Greeks and Turks. Our conversation was filled with democracy, church-state countries that are fraught with difficulties, and man's creation. He was a very educated professor for a Kentucky University, but he was the only one from his family who left Cypress. Soon, he would have to fulfill a mandatory two-year service in the Turkish Cypress Army. His heart was heavy with the potential of being separated from his work at the university, but he knew this obligation was the price he paid for the freedom of his family back in Cypress. The taxi driver's accent revealed his Haitian background. We spoke of Haiti, its problems, and challenges. We also spoke of my work with Pastor Israel Isidor, his orphanage, his school, and his parish. This friendly conversation made me realize how gracious God had been throughout my deployment and homecoming and calmed my anxiety about the upcoming interviews.

Walking about between these behemoth buildings, in their shadows and their glorious height, I was filled with interesting stories as I strode along in my DCUs. Stopping at a cigar store on Fifth Avenue, I struck up a conversation with one of the shopkeepers. Discussed were not only cigars but religion, faith, and morality. Upon knowing that I was a Lutheran chaplain, he pointed me to seek out one of the other shopkeepers who was also a Lutheran. Greeting him and sharing the peace of the Lord with him brought him joy during such a busy and difficult time. The strike of the Mass Transit Authority workers had created a great amount of difficulty in order to get into work, and all the businesses within Manhattan shared this hardship due to the reduced number of customers and the reduced number of workers.

Training on how to handle the media and their questions was the next adventure in the Big Apple. The army contracts a public relations firm who handles such training for novices such as me. How fascinating to learn about the workings of television and the interviews that are produced on them. After several practice sessions, we were more confident of our camera presence and the ability to handle questions from the fray of controversy. Our first assignment was to tape a segment with CNN to be aired five days later. After the obligatory makeup session, we entered the inner sanctum of the studio, where Kitty Pilgrim interviewed us. It went well, and the edited version that as shown was thankfully very complimentary of us. Next, we walked to the FOX News center and waited our turn to be interviewed with Dave Asmus. Prior to our big debut on live national news, we exchanged pleasantries with Steve Forbes; surreal, to say the least. Dave's questions came very quick and staccato, so it gave urgency to compact all that we needed to share in a very concise fashion lest we succumb to the dreaded "Uhs" of desperately seeking the right words. Surprisingly, our session again went smoothly, and we were quite warmly received by the host. Then, just as quickly as this day of exposure to national media began, it ended. Time to go home and bask in God's grace, the completion of my year of hope, and in the presence of my beloveds.

Author's note: Upon my return to Austin, I was greeted by the "biggest yellow ribbon in Texas" wrapped lovingly around the fifty-foot high bell tower of St. Paul Lutheran Church. In addition, the trees and grounds surrounding the church were all decked out in yellow ribbons, one hundred US flags, and welcome home signs. The support from these caring and devoted people comforted me and my family while I was deployed. Their welcome home amazed and humbled me. I am only a man and a sinner at that. But God has shown me love and grace beyond measure, and I can only but give Him my thanks and praise.

www.ingramcontent.com/pod-product-compliance
Lightning Source LLC
Chambersburg PA
CBHW050031040726
47599CB00015B/1627